100 YEARS OF THE RAF 1918-2018

Warners Group Publications,
The Maltings, West Street,
Bourne, Lincolnshire PE10 9PH
Tel: 01778 391000 • Fax: 01778 392422

Publisher Rob McDonnell
robm@warnersgroup.co.uk

Editor Duncan Evans
duncane@warnersgroup.co.uk
Tel: 01778 391103

Contributors Chris Duffill, Tim Heath, Geoff Puddefoot, Martin Taylor, Mark Simner, Ben Rawlings, Matt Moss, Barry Wheeler, Jarrod Cotter, Garrett Eriksen, Ed Hallet

Head of Design and Production
Lynn Wright

Designer
Mike Edwards

ADVERTISING
Group Key Account Manager
Claire Ingram
claire.ingram@warnersgroup.co.uk
Tel: 01778 391179

Sales Executive Ben Jackson
ben.jackson@warnersgroup.co.uk
Tel: 01778 391129

Auction House Sales Executive
Kristina Green
kristina.green@warnersgroup.co.uk
Tel: 01778 390296

Advertising Production & Design
Nicola Lock
nicola.lock@warnersgroup.co.uk

DISTRIBUTION
Warners Distribution
Andy Perry • Tel: 01778 391152

MARKETING
Marketing Brand Manager
Nicola Lumb

Marketing Assistant
Katherine Brown

This publication is printed by Warners 01778 395111

Reproduction in whole or in part without written permission is prohibited. All rights reserved. Dates, information and prices quoted are believed to be correct at time of going to press but are subject to change and no responsibility is accepted for any errors or omissions. Neither the editor nor the publisher accept responsibility for any material submitted, whether photographic or otherwise. While we endeavour to ensure that firms and organisations mentioned are reputable, the Editor can give no guarantee that they will fulfil their obligations under all circumstances. Whilst every care has been taken to compile current valuations, the publishers cannot accept liability for loss, financial or otherwise, incurred by reliance placed on the information herein. Quoted prices are indicative and are for illustrative purposes only. Always seek expert advice with regard to valuations. DISCLAIMER: The views expressed by contributors and advertisers are not necessarily those of the publishers. Every care is taken to ensure that the contents of the magazine are accurate but the publishers cannot accept responsibility for errors. While reasonable care is taken when accepting advertisements, the publishers cannot accept any responsibility for any resulting unsatisfactory transactions. They will however investigate any written complaints.

WELCOME

Almost 100 years ago the Great War was coming to an end and the two competing air forces – the Royal Flying Corps and the Royal Naval Air Service – were merged to form the Royal Air Force. April 2018 is the 100th anniversary of that coming together and to celebrate we'd like to introduce you to this special, one-off magazine, *100 Years of the RAF*.

Within these pages you'll discover the history of the RAF, how that amalgamation went ahead and how the service developed leading up to its greatest challenge – the dark days of the Battle of Britain. Having defeated the Luftwaffe and stalled any plans of invasion, Churchill declared, on 20 August 1940, that, "Never was so much owed by so many to so few." After the biggest conflict the world had ever seen, the role of the RAF changed again, to counter the nuclear threat in the Cold War. War was to break out again though, this time in the South Atlantic as Argentina invaded the Falkland Islands. Finally, our historical tour takes in the Gulf War and modern developments.

During those 100 years many people have influenced how the RAF flew and worked so, in our next section, Heroes of the RAC/RAF, we look at figures such as Viscount Hugh Trenchard, popularly known as the Father of the RAF, RJ Mitchell, the designer of the Spitfire, legendary pilots like Douglas Bader and unheralded figures like Pauline Gower of the ATA.

Airbases come and go, depending on the needs of the RAF and the military and political situation, but some names are etched in history forever. Discover the stories of RAF Uxbridge, Biggin Hill, Manston and Brize Norton, what they did in the past and what the future holds.

What makes the RAF special, in many people's eyes, are the aircraft. From the classic biplane, the Sopwith Camel of WWI, to the ultimate piston-engine fighter, the Supermarine Spitfire. These are the airborne chariots, piloted by chivalrous heroes, that legends are made of. Come then, and discover the stories of the Mosquito, Lancaster, the mighty Vulcan and the ultra-modern Eurofighter Typhoon in the Iconic Aircraft section.

To round off this celebration of the 100th anniversary of the RAF, it's time to take a look at the RAF of today, from the current air power strategy and careers in the RAF, to a look at the memorials to the fallen, the airshows and museums where you can see RAF aircraft up close, as well as how to get into collecting RAF militaria.

And finally, if you've enjoyed this special publication then how about a chance to win a ride in a Lancaster bomber yourself? That's the prize being offered by the Lincs Aviation Heritage Centre at East Kirkby, in our exclusive competition on page 131.

Duncan Evans,
Editor

CONTENTS

62

50

History
OF THE RAF

Your guide to how the RAF was created and successfully fought WWII, to preparing for Soviet aggression and then tackling the Argentines, thousands of miles away.

Heroes
OF THE RAC/RAF

The people who made the Air Force what it is today, from designers and fighter aces, to commanders and those who changed attitudes.

Iconic
AIRCRAFT

From Sopwith Camels dogfighting over the trenches to long-range missile attacks with the latest technology of the Eurofighter Typhoon, these are the iconic aircraft that have served the RAF well for the last 100 years.

66

106

Airbases
PAST & PRESENT

This is where the men and women of the RAF served and flew from. Discover what happened at these famous air bases, what roles they performed and what has happened to them now.

The RAF
TODAY

So we come to the present and what the RAF is doing today. Here you can learn about the military strategy, as well as discovering what careers are available. Then you can attend one of the many memorials around the country, visit airshows and museums, or start collecting RAF militaria.

124

WIN!
A RIDE IN A
LANCASTER
SEE PAGE 131

Auctioneers C&T Valuers

Regular Auctions of Military & Aviation Collectables Held Throughout The Year

the saleroom The home of art & antiques auctions   **Live Online Bidding**   invaluable

Auctioneers C&T Valuers

Unit 4, High House Business Park, Kenardington, NR Ashford, Kent TN26 2LF

Please contact Matthew Tredwen :
Tel: +44 (0) 1233 510050   Email: matthew.tredwen@candtauctions.co.uk

www.candtauctions.co.uk

THE EARLY YEARS OF THE ROYAL AIR FORCE

How the Royal Flying Corps and Royal Naval Air Service came to create the RAF

Words Tim Heath

Man's mastery of the skies can be dated back to December 17 1903 when American born brother's Wilbur and Orville Wright constructed and flew the first powered aircraft. Many early aircraft designs evolved around the bi-plane principle constructed of wood, wire and fabric. The engines which powered these early aeroplanes were relatively simple often unreliable and featured poor performance. It was in this guise that the aeroplane was first used in what would soon become termed as 'aerial warfare'.

The first aviator to fly an aeroplane in an offensive role was Italian pilot Lieutenant Giulio Gavotti. During fighting in November 1911, between Italy and forces, Gavotti took off in an Austrian-built Taub (Dove) monoplane to drop bombs on Turkish forces. The bombs were in the form of one kilogram grenades which would be thrown from his aircraft once over the Turkish troop positions. Prior to Lieutenant Gavotti's first offensive flight aircraft were only previously used in the aerial reconnaissance role. Although Gavotti's mission was described as a success by the Italian tabloids it is doubtful as to whether many casualties were caused to the Turks. It did however prove to the watching world that aircraft could be used to carry out attacks on an enemy force. The British were not slow in noticing the possible value of aircraft for military use particularly for the reconnaissance and artillery spotting role. The Committee of Imperial Defence established a sub-committee in November 1911 specifically to question the validity of

Giulio Gavotti was the first aviator to fly an aeroplane in an offensive role

military aviation. On 28 February 1912 the sub-committee recommended that a Flying Corps be created. The Flying Corps should consist of a naval wing, a military wing, a central flying training school and an aircraft production facility. The recommendations of the sub-committee were accepted and on 13 April 1912 King George V signed a Royal warrant establishing the Royal Flying Corps. The RFC's motto was 'Per ardua ad astra', or Through adversity to the stars) and its initial allowed strength was 133 officers, 12

The engines which powered these early aeroplanes were relatively simple

manned balloons and 36 aircraft.

Originally under the responsibility of Brigadier General Henderson, the Director of military training, Major Sykes was Commander of the military wing while Commander C.R Samson led the naval wing. The Royal Navy was of the view that their air force faced differing and more unique challenges to those faced by the military wing and wishing to retain more control over its aircraft formally separated its branch, renaming it the Royal Naval Air Service. In 1913 a base for seaplanes was approved for construction on the Isle of Grain and for an airship base at Kingsnorth. The RNAS pioneered the concept of flying aircraft from ships at sea. The first RNAS pilot to fly an aircraft from a ship under way was none other than Commander C. Samson who flew a modified Shorts S38 hydro-aeroplane off HMS Hibernia. Such experimentation would ultimately lead to the revolutionary naval aviation concept of the aircraft carrier which would prove a decisive weapon in many future conflicts. By June 1914, 44 officers and 105 other ranks of the RNAS had been trained at the Central Flying School and a further 35 officers and men had been trained in airship work. The RFC was to suffer its first fatal crash on 5 July 1912 when Pilot Captain Eustace B Loraine and his observer Staff Sergeant R.H.V Wilson were lost when their aircraft crashed near Stonehenge on Salisbury Plain. An order was issued that all flying should continue despite the tragedy - thus a tradition began.

With the outbreak of war with Germany in August 1914 the RFC was organised into a system of A, B and C flights. The RFC flights consisted of four to six aircraft each depending on squadron strength, aircraft serviceability etc. Full strength squadrons of 18 aircraft were feasible. Squadron Commanding Officers generally held rank of Major while Flight Commanders were usually Captains. Using the aircraft they had in service at the time primarily for the reconnaissance role patrols could be in the air for up to two hours at a time. A RFC pilot would serve a continuous six month period of duty followed by a period of up to three months leave. The balloons in service under the RFC were used for the static observation of enemy movements on the field of battle. The balloon crews also faced great dangers in their duties as they became a prime target for enemy fighter aircraft.

The general organisation of the RNAS followed a similar formula to that of the RFC. Prior to WWI experiments had been undertaken with the arming of aircraft. Initially lightweight rifle calibre machineguns were trialled in a number of aircraft types to ascertain their suitability. The problems were almost immediately obvious before the aircraft had even left the ground. The ideal concept was to have any weapon firing forward yet, at this early stage, there was no means of firing through the arc of the moving propeller. The construction of early aircraft, even with rearward firing weapons, meant that it would have been all too easy to shoot parts of the aircraft away. The wings and maze of struts and bracing wires prevalent in these early designs meant that any arc of fire was extremely limited. At this stage of WWI it was not uncommon for rival British and German reconnaissance aircrews to encounter one another in the air exchanging nothing more malicious than a smile, wave or the odd obscenity. This however would soon change as measures were discussed at how one might combat an enemy machine. As many of the early RFC aircraft were two seaters (pilot and observer) it would be the observer who would, at least initially,

The Focker EII Eindecker

Men of No. 1 Squadron RNAS 1914

Mick Mannock, WWI ace

The general organisation of the RNAS followed a similar formula to that of the RFC

take up the offensive/defensive role. As a result some unorthodox practices came to fruition. Grenades were taken up into aircraft where they could be thrown at an enemy machine and shotguns were also used though it's doubtful that either would have proved effective at all but the very closest of ranges. RFC observers tried small arms such as pistols and rifles but the pistol proved far too inaccurate and the single shot rifles too slow and therefore too unlikely to score a hit. The whole concept of air warfare would change on 5 October 1914 when

French pilot, Louis Quenault, opened fire on a German aircraft for the first time with a machine gun. The breakthrough for the RFC came with the Vickers FB.5 in February 1915, along with the FE.2B and Airco DH.1. All these aircraft had rearward fitted engines operating in the pusher fashion. This meant that there was a forward position ahead of the pilot where an observer could be placed with a forward firing machine gun offering a respectable field of fire. That said the performance of the early pusher concept RFC fighters was not impressive and by late WWI they were simply far too underpowered to catch their quarry.

The real revolution with respect to the fighter aircraft came in mid-1915 when the German single seat monoplane fighter the Fokker Eindecker first appeared in the skies over France. The Fokker Eindecker had a monoplane configuration, an engine delivering a top speed of 87mph and a forward firing machine gun that fired through the arc of the propeller, aimed and fired by the pilot himself. It was only a matter of time before an example of this new fighter would fall into British hands.

The excellent S.E.5 was quick and able to turn tightly in a dogfight

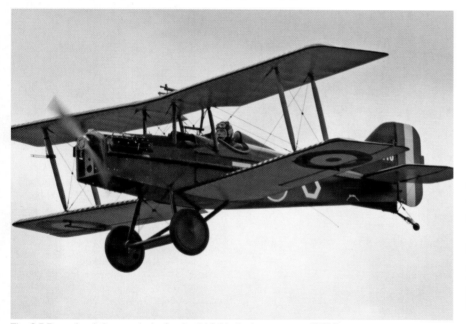

The S.E.5 regained air superiority for the RAC for the latter years of WWI

Lt William Leefe Robinson shooting down a German Zeppelin

Lieutenant William Leefe Robinson VC - the first person to shoot down a Zeppelin

In August 1915 the RNAS came officially under the control of the Royal Navy

When the new technology was presented to the British the machine gun synchronisation was replicated for use in the RFC. Though the Fokker Eindecker would enjoy a period of air superiority over the RFC through a time known as the 'Fokker Scourge' this technical advantage was brief.

At the outbreak of hostilities in August 1914 the RNAS had 93 aircraft, six airships, two balloons and 727 personnel at its disposal. In August 1915 the RNAS came officially under the control of the Royal Navy. The RNAS role was similar to that of

the RFC and not exclusively sea based. The RNAS had aircraft capable of taking off from vessels which had been specially adapted for the task, float planes which were able to land on the sea and in this role they carried out maritime patrol and reconnaissance duties. These duties entailed coastal patrols locating and attacking enemy shipping and submarines. The RNAS was equipped with notable bi-plane aircraft such as the Airco DH.4, Airco DH.6, and Airco DH.9.

As WWI progressed the RNAS, like the RFC, had an extensive fleet of maritime

fighter and bomber aircraft at its disposal. With varying configurations of armament from forward firing synchronised machine guns to bombs and torpedoes it was becoming a formidable force the importance of which would not be fully recognised until World War II. During the precarious early years, methods for attacking enemy shipping and submarines remained both rudimentary and risky. Bombing techniques slowly evolved from that of an observer manually dropping a relatively small explosive device onto a target to that of

Mounting a gun to the front of the aeroplane

A Lewis gun on a Foster mounting fitted to an Avro 504K Night Fighter

Modern replicas of WWI bi-planes can be seen in action at airshows around the country

The early years of flight - just keeping off the ground was a challenge

Sopwith Camel F-1 with twin guns

larger explosives being carried beneath the wings or fuselage of an aircraft, the device being aimed through a periscope sight and released via a simple mechanical mechanism operated by the observer. There was still much to learn on the mathematical principles of ballistics involving the correct delivery of airborne munitions. The rapid development brought about by the war time situation meant that an understanding of the theories was imperative if an aircrew were to be successful in air combat, whether involved in ground attack or bombing or indeed air to air warfare. Soon techniques were learned and being taught in the training schools. All of these skills would be crucial elements in future conflicts around the world and aircrews of the RFC and RNAS would become amongst the most proficient and professional of their kind.

Basic air to air combat during WWI was an exceptionally dangerous, brutal unforgiving business where the loser faced certain death. There were no parachutes that could be relied upon to save an airman's life should his aircraft be shot down or become unserviceable for whatever reason.

Methods devised by pilots of both sides included attacking from above and from out of the sun

If an aircraft was not too badly damaged or had suffered technical problems with its engine(s), the pilot, if skilled or lucky enough, might get his aircraft down and land in one piece, though more often than not this was not the case. In many instances, when an airman was shot down in combat he would be fully conscious in his, often flaming, aircraft right up until the moment he impacted the ground which, in some cases, could be several minutes.

The tactics devised for fighter versus fighter engagements had to be learned

through hard experience. Methods devised by pilots of both sides included attacking from above an opponent and from out of the sun, attacking from the rear and below in the opponents blind spot. Other complex maneuverers were soon introduced and taught in the flying schools but success depended largely upon the skill of the pilot. The improving quality of aircraft coming into service for both the RFC and RNAS coupled with a good understanding of tactics meant that 'Aces' were soon born. The Germans had already set standards in air warfare that would soon be emulated by their enemies.

With the arrival in service of aircraft such as the Royal Aircraft Factory S.E.5 biplane fighter which entered service with the RFC in March 1917 were at least able to match the excellence of the German fighter pilots. The S.E.5 (Scout Experimental) was an aircraft specifically designed with a 'green' pilot in mind. It was easy to fly and carried an armament of a single 7.7mm Vickers machine gun fixed to fire forward above the engine and a synchronised weapon to fire through the propeller via a Constantinesco

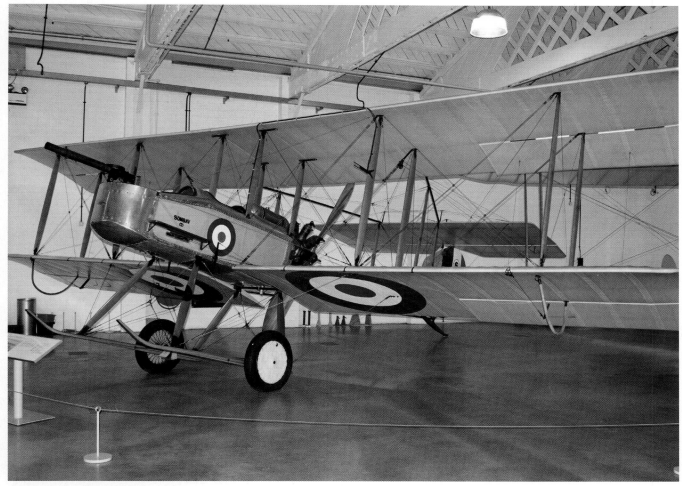

A replica of the Vickers FB.5 Gunbus

The gunner of a Blackburn Perth with a 37mm automatic cannon installation

interrupter mechanism. There was also provision for a 7.7mm Lewis drum fed machine gun on a Foster mounting on the upper wing. This weapon was reloaded by the pilot who had to pull the weapon down on a rail to attach a fresh ammunition magazine. The S.E.5 could also carry four external bombs, depending on the tactical requirements of a mission.

The S.E.5 was without doubt one of the most capable fighters in use with the RFC in WWI. It became the preferred mount of RFC Aces such as Billy Bishop VC, CB, DSO & Bar, MC, DFC, ED who was credited with 72 victories, Cecil Lewis MC, credited with eight victories and Edward Corringham 'Mick' Mannock VC, DSO, & two bars, MC & bar, credited with 61 victories.

Mannock was, without doubt, one of the most successful British fighter pilots of WWI and a master tactician. He introduced 15 rules to be followed by a pilot in air combat. Included were that pilots should attack with zest, and must hold their fire until they get within 100yrd of the target, achieve surprise by approaching from the east (German side of the front), utilise the

Mannock was, without doubt, one of the most successful British pilots of WWI

glare of the sun and cloud cover to achieve surprise, keep turning in a dog fight and never fly straight unless he is firing his guns. Edward 'Mick' Mannock's remarkable, and valuable, service with the RFC came to a premature end when on 26 July 1918, after shooting down an enemy two-seater behind the German front-line, Mannock is believed to have dived down to view the wreckage of his victim, breaking one of the unwritten rules of fellow pilots. While crossing the trenches his aircraft was met with a large volley of fire from the ground. Mannock's

Two man Airco Dh.4 waiting to take off

Airco de Havilland DH.4 in the skies over the Western Front in 1918

aircraft was hit and immediately caught fire, crashing into the ground behind the German lines.

Both the RFC and RNAS also had the task of intercepting the German Zeppelin menace which first appeared in the dark skies over England in January 1915. Early attempts at shooting down German Zeppelin airships appeared futile. Yet on the night and early morning of 2/3 September 1916 Lieutenant William Leefe Robinson became the first RFC pilot to do so. As technology in the RFC's fighter arm increased so did that of the earliest attempts at strategic bombing. The Handley Page Type O which first flew on 17 December 1915 was, at the time, one of the largest aircraft in the world. It entered service with the RFC in 1916 where it was used in France for tactical night attacks on targets in German occupied France and Belgium. It was also used in the strategic bombing of industrial targets in the German Rhineland. The RNAS were also supplied with the Handley Page Type O where it became the ideal platform for carrying out anti-submarine reconnaissance and bombing in the Tees estuary.

On 1 April 1918 the Royal Flying Corps was merged with the Royal Naval Air Service to create the Royal Air Force. There is no doubt that both the RFC and RNAS were both major components in the defeat of Imperial Germany in the 1914-1918 Great War. Much of what had been learned during those hard years of war should have been nurtured and developed in the years after 1918. Sadly it would appear that an air of complacency clouded the judgement of the powers that be in the tentative years of peace that followed Germany's defeat.

After 1918 the pace of aircraft development in the UK for the RAF seemed to fall into a lull. The RAF was still largely equipped with bi-plane fighter aircraft well into the 1930s. Although many of these aircraft possessed far superior performance, firepower and agility to their WWI predecessors, they would be totally inadequate for the next arena of battle which would be World War II.

While the Schneider Trophy for

On 1 April 1918 the Royal Flying Corps was merged with the Royal Naval Air Service

seaplanes had been in existence from 1912, created to encourage technical advances in civil aviation, the races certainly grew in popularity throughout the 1930s. For the British, Reginald John Mitchell, of the Supermarine Company, developed the Supermarine S.6B seaplane to compete in the 1931 races. Mitchells design theory was cutting edge for the day and he was known as a perfectionist in his design work, always seeking less than obvious solutions to any technical problems he encountered.

The S.6B would be powered by an engine which would become a household name in the coming years - the Rolls Royce R which possessed 2,350 horsepower. In the event, the Supermarine S.6B proved to be a giant leap forward in aircraft technology, winning the Schneider Trophy for Britain and setting a speed record of 407mph. This was the fastest aircraft in the world at the time. Mitchell was a remarkable man and not one to rest on his laurels. As the dark clouds of war again began to gather on the horizon he would be able to apply all he learned from the Schneider Trophy into the design of

Reginald John Mitchell designer of the Supermarine SF and the legendary Spitfire

military aircraft.

With the resurgence of German aggression in Europe, Mitchell knew that time was running out and that if the RAF were to succeed in defending Britain's shores from, what was at the time, the most powerful enemy it would face in her history, then the RAF would need a fighter aircraft that could take on the best the enemy could field. Many remarkable aircraft began to roll off the drawing boards but perhaps the most iconic would be the Supermarine Spitfire. Mitchell died due to illness before he could see the prototype fly but his legendary fighter, along with the Hawker Hurricane, would become symbols of the RAF that would endure for eternity.

Newark Air Museum
Make a date for our 2018 Special Events

SATURDAY 3RD MARCH, 2018
Indoor Aeroboot /
Aerojumble Aviation &
Avionic sale

SUNDAY 1ST APRIL, 2018
100th Anniversary of
RAF Open Cockpits
Day

SUNDAY 8TH APRIL, 2018
RAF Balderton Reunion
& Book Launch

SATURDAY 19TH MAY, 2018
Tribute to the V Force
Reunion

**SATURDAY 23RD & SUNDAY 24TH
JUNE, 2018**
Cockpit-Fest & Aeroboot

**SATURDAY 11TH & SUNDAY 12TH
AUGUST, 2018**
1940s Weekend

**SATURDAY 1ST & SUNDAY 2ND
SEPTEMBER, 2018**
Shackleton Boys Book
Launch

SATURDAY 13TH OCTOBER, 2018
Indoor Aeroboot /
Aerojumble Aviation &
Avionic sale

NEWARK AIR MUSEUM
The friendly aviation museum

Drove Lane, Winthorpe, Newark, Notts, NG24 2NY Tel: 01636 707170
Email: enquire@newarkairmuseum.org   Follow us on Twitter: @NewarkAirMus

www.newarkairmuseum.org

The museum is a registered charity no. 256434

THE RAF IN WWII

How the Battle of Britain was won and taking the fight to Germany

Words Gerald Prenderghast

When Britain declared war on Nazi Germany in August 1939, the RAF had already gone some way towards meeting the imminent threat, with an establishment of 157 squadrons and 3,700 aircraft, many of them modern fighters such as the Hurricane and Spitfire. The first primitive radar installations, Chain Home, were already integrated with the RAF sector control rooms and the Observer Corps to direct fighter operations and, unlike the *Luftwaffe,* the RAF had medium bombers such as the Vickers Wellington capable of reaching the industrial centre of Germany on the Ruhr, with even better, long range heavy bombers in the process of development.

Expansion was not just limited to aircraft. It also incorporated the Air Commonwealth Training Plan, an ambitious aircrew training initiative agreed in 1939, that recruited suitable candidates from Britain, the Commonwealth and the United States, finally resulting in 168,000 trained aircrew. Experienced Polish, Czech, Irish, American and French aircrew also joined the RAF, along with flyers of other nationalities who had all managed to escape from Hitler's Fortress Europe.

Between 1939 and 1945, 180,000 aircrew served in the RAF which, with the additional ground staff, were organised into three major administrative and strategic divisions: Fighter Command, Bomber Command and Coastal Command.

RAF Fighter Command

Responsible for home defence and later attacks on Germany's European defences. Commanded between 1939 and 1945 by:
Sir Hugh Dowding
(June 1939-November 1940)
Sir Sholto Douglas
(November 1940-November 1942)
Trafford Leigh-Mallory
(November 1942-November 1943)
Sir Roderic Hill
(November 1943-May 1945)

RAF HQ was Bentley Priory in North London and the service was divided into

6 Groups (9 Group – 14 Group), each one having responsibility for the defence of a different section of the country. Groups were commanded by Air Vice-Marshals and within the operational area of each Group were a number of Sector Stations which, as well as housing operational squadrons, also contained the Sector Control Rooms which directed RAF fighter sorties.
Aircraft operated during WWII included:
Hawker Hurricane
(14,583 built): Introduced into RAF; 1937
Supermarine Spitfire
(20,351 built): Introduced into RAF; 1938
Bristol Beaufighter
(5,928 built): Introduced into RAF; 1940
de Havilland Mosquito
(7,781 built): Introduced into RAF; 1941
Hawker Tempest
(1,702 built): Introduced into RAF; 1944

In 1943, Fighter Command was reorganised into two sections, the Second Tactical Air Force, which concentrated on supporting ground forces after the eventual invasion of Europe, and Air Defence of Great Britain (ADGB). The primary role of ADGB was defending the UK from attack, in a role exactly similar to the original Fighter Command, and this was acknowledged in 1944, when the group was once again renamed Fighter Command.

RAF Bomber Command

Bomber command oversaw bomber operations against enemy targets, including special operations. Between 1940 and 1945 it was commanded by:
Air Marshal Charles Portal
(April 1940-October 1940)
Sir Richard Peirse
(October 1940-January 1942)
Air Chief Marshal Sir Arthur (Bomber) Harris
(February 1942-September 1945).

The command was divided initially into 5 Groups (1 Group-5 Group), although other Groups having specific roles were added later. The aircraft operated during WWII included these:
Armstrong Whitworth Whitley
(1,814 built): Introduced into RAF; 1937
Vickers Wellington (11,462 built):
Introduced into RAF; 1938
Handley Page Halifax (6,176 built):
Introduced into RAF; 1940
Avro Lancaster (7,377 built):
Introduced into RAF; 1942

1939-1942: Early problems and the beginning of strategic bombing

At the beginning of WWII, Bomber Command was considerably handicapped both by having too few aircraft to operate as a successful independent strategic force and restrictions on targets which might result in civilian casualties. It was also at a disadvantage technically, having no airborne radar and an inaccurate bomb sight. Fighter Command was better supplied with aircraft, although replacement of damaged aircraft was not rapid and pilots also suffered from inadequate rest periods and lack of replacements. Coastal Command was perhaps worst treated, with poor training facilities and aircrew shortages lasting until 1942, when it was able to begin its own war against the U-boats.

Bomber Command's first target of the war, on 3 and 4 September 1939, were a number of German warships in harbour. There followed a series of desultory monthly bombing raids, until target restrictions were lifted on 15 May 1940, one day after the *Luftwaffe* bombed the civilian population of Rotterdam. On 16 May 1940 the RAF began attacking targets in the Ruhr Area which included oil plants and other civilian industrial targets, although by now the Battle of France had already begun and some of Bomber Command's scanty resources needed to be apportioned to support British forces retreating to the coast and who would soon be part of the Dunkirk evacuation (Operation *Dynamo*).

Dunkirk

An RAF contingent had arrived in France to support the BEF before the beginning of the German Offensive on 10 May 1940. Commanded by Air Marshall Arthur Barr and designated British Air Forces in France, the RAF units under Barrat were divided into the Air Component, providing fighter cover and reconnaissance for the BEF, and the AASF (Advanced Air Striking Force), operating the bombers.

Unfortunately, the RAF bombers proved vulnerable to German fighters and the *Wehrmacht's* disciplined ground fire, the AASF losing 63 bombers between the beginning of operations on the 10 May and 13 May. In the face of these deadly German attacks and the *Wehrmacht's* advance, the AASF combined its depleted squadrons and flew only night bombing and reconnaissance operations. While carrying out these sorties, the squadrons moved towards the coast from where they returned to Britain on 15 May. The fighters remained in France until 18 May or relocated to the Channel islands, from where they attempted to cover the evacuation, although the *Luftwaffe* were so numerous that the RAF could not halt the carnage on the beaches and the Spitfire

1. Map of radar coverage of Britain by Chain Home radar stations, in August 1941 **2.** RAF personnel being evacuated from Dunkirk **3.** Crew and seaplane from Coastal Command

Aircraft operated during WWII included:
Bristol Beaufort
(1,121 built): Introduced into RAF; 1939
Short Sunderland
(777 built): Introduced into RAF; 1938
Lockheed Hudson
(2,941 built): Introduced into RAF; 1939
Consolidated PBY Catalina
(3,305 built): Introduced into RAF; 1941

RAF Coastal Command

Tasked with protecting Allied sea-borne trade, attacking enemy shipping and air-sea rescue of downed pilots and sailors. Commanded between 1937 and 1945 by:
Air Marshal Sir Frederick Bowhill
(August 1937-June1941)
Air Chief Marshal Sir Philip Joubert de la Ferté (June 1941-February 1943)
Sir John Slessor
(February 1943-January 1944)
Sir William Sholto Douglas
(January 1944-June 1945)

Although Coastal Command never received the accolades awarded to other units of the RAF, they were still doing essential work. Between 1941 and 1945, Coastal Command logged over one million flying hours during 240,000 operations, sinking 212 U-boats and 366 German merchant ships, for the loss of 2,060 aircraft and 5,866 personnel killed in action. In their rescue operations Coastal Command picked up 10,663 persons, including Allied crews, enemy personnel and merchant sailors.

and Hurricane reinforcements flying from England had only enough fuel to remain over Dunkirk for 10 minutes.

Battle of Britain and the Blitz

By 4 June 1940, most of the BEF had been evacuated from Dunkirk and the mood in Britain had changed from black despair to one of exuberant cheerfulness. Churchill soon tempered this wave of optimism, when he delivered a speech in the House of Commons on 4 June, reminding the British that, "We must be very careful not to assign to this deliverance the attributes of a victory. Wars are not won by evacuations."

On the 18 June he made matters even plainer, saying, "What General Weygand has called the Battle of France is over. The Battle of Britain is about to begin."

Hitler had made a number of attempts, after the invasion of Poland, to arrive at a peaceful settlement with Britain and when he ordered the *Luftwaffe* to begin their cycle of raids on 26 June 1940, his Directives indicate that it was done to secure a peaceful settlement, rather than an occupation of the British Isles. Consequently, the Battle was initially one of attrition, intended to incapacitate the RAF, leaving Britain no defence against air attack and forced to begin peace negotiations. Despite its highly publicised preparations, Operation *Sealion* was a last resort, German naval officers being well aware of the difficulties inherent in an invasion of Britain.

The Battle of Britain

Five main phases in the Battle are usually identified by historians, although authorities differ as to the actual dates. Those given here originate from the Royal Air Force Museum:
26 June – 16 July: *Störangriffe* (Nuisance Raids), scattered, relatively light raids involving small numbers of aircraft during both day and night.
17 July – 12 August: Daylight *Kanalkampf* (Shipping) attacks now intensified, as did attacks against ports, coastal airfields and night raids on RAF stations and aircraft manufacturing centres.
13 August – 6 September: *Adlerangriff* (Eagle Attack), the main assault intended to to destroy the RAF in southern England with intensive daylight attacks on airfields. This proved unsuccessful, so in an attempt to draw the fighters out, heavy night bombing of ports and industrial cities followed, beginning on 19 August.
7 September – 2 October: The Blitz begins, with continual day and night raids on London and other cities.
3 October – 31 October: Large scale night bombing raids, mostly on London, also daylight attacks intended to lure RAF fighters into dogfights.

The *Luftwaffe* began conducting nuisance

Number of squadrons	Aircraft type	Role
8	Fairey Battle	Light bomber
2	Bristol Blenheim	Medium bomber
6	Hawker Hurricane	Fighter

RAF aircraft deployed to France in 1940

Number of squadrons	Aircraft type	Role
5	Westland Lysander	Tactical reconnaissance and photographic survey
4	Bristol Blenheim	Strategic reconnaissance
4	Hawker Hurricane	Fighter

AASF
Total aircraft deployed to France by RAF: 680 fighters and 392 bombers.
Total Luftwaffe aircraft deployed during the Battle of France: 5,100 fighters and bombers.

raids against Britain on 5 May, in order to give their bomber crews the chance to train under battle conditions and discover the best bomb load which achieved maximum effect, such small raids increasing in intensity from 18 May, when 100 bombers attacked Kent and Yorkshire. However, the British were also able to use this breathing space between Dunkirk and the beginning of larger raids to train their own pilots and anti-aircraft crews as well as being able to assess German tactics.

The RAF also began night raids against military objectives and airfields in German towns on 11 May, although they had little success and many of the Bristol Blenheims

3

4

sent on these operations were shot down, in some cases whole squadrons being lost to the Bf 109s. However, on 7 September the threat of invasion caused both Bomber and Coastal Commands to begin attacks on Channel ports and these were more successful, over 200 barges of the invasion fleet being sunk, which may have helped persuade Hitler to cancel *Sealion* indefinitely. Attacks on British shipping had also begun alongside the nuisance raids but from the middle of July these raids intensified and produced a steady drain of ships and their covering aircraft.

Overestimates of British losses by *Luftwaffe* intelligence now led Goering to believe that both the nuisance raids and shipping battles had reduced RAF numbers sufficiently to make their airfields an easy target. Consequently, on 6 August he implemented a strategy which was intended to destroy 11 Group, defending Kent and Essex, followed by 12 and 13 Groups, so that bombing of military and economic targets could proceed unhindered over Britain, culminating in a major bombing attack on London. The main attack was designated

1. Member of Observer Corps on duty in Central London during the Battle of Britain. Later in the war OC. personnel were supplied with uniforms
2. Junkers Ju 88, twin-engined medium bomber. With the same range as the He 111 but a better bomb load, this aircraft proved useful in the raids of 1940 **3.** Messerschmidt Bf 109 G10 parked on the grass bordering a landing strip. This is a later, faster version of the aircraft which operated against the Allies during the Battle of Britain (Used under GFDL)
4. Production line building the Bf 109

	Participating aircrew	Dead/wounded/ missing or captured	Aircraft in service	Aircraft destroyed
RAF	5,000	1612/422/0	1,963	1,744
Luftwaffe	7,500	2,585/735/ 925	2,550	1,977

Fighter Command and Luftwaffe casualties during the Battle of Britain. 1 July-7 September 1940

Total aircrew includes fighters, bombers, reconnaissance and Coastal Command aircraft.

1. A row of newly delivered de Havilland Mosquitos **2.** Film from Spitfires camera gun film showing passage of tracer ammunition towards enemy aircraft **3.** A Supermarine Spitfire, this is FVBBM597 of the Historic Aircraft Collection (Used under GFDL)

Adlerangriff (Eagle Attack), with the first day of offensive operations termed Adlertag *(Eagle Day)*.

Bad weather delayed Eagle Day until 13 August, although attacks on the radar stations began on the 12 August, resulting in three being taken off the air briefly, although all were working again within six hours. This revealed the lack of practical intelligence available to the *Luftwaffe,* since they targeted the robust radar towers and not the power and telephone lines from the sector stations, which would have made much better strategic targets. Between 13 and 15 August, the *Luftwaffe* attacked coastal airfields, some of the smaller satellite air stations and made further raids on the radar chain as well as mounting the highest number of sorties on a single day of the Battle on 15 August. This included an attack by *Luftflotte 5* (Air Fleet 5) on northern England, resulting in the loss of 23 aircraft out of total of 150 sent on the raid. In another underestimate by German Intelligence, it was suggested that the RAF had only 300 serviceable fighters left by 17 August, although the actual figure was 1438 serviceable machines, twice those available in July 1940. Misled by this optimistic intelligence, Goering gave orders to destroy the RAF's main airfields in Kent and attacks began in the early afternoon of 18 August. Despite some German successes in both the air raids and ensuing dogfights, when the Bf 109s began to withdraw after using all their fuel, the RAF pounced, shooting down so many of the unwieldy Messerschmitt Bf110 fighters and Ju-87 Stuka dive bombers, that the Stukas were never used again in attacks on Britain. By 6.30pm darkness was falling and the attacks were losing their initial intensity, only five bomber groups

being sent against non-military targets in Essex and the Midlands. Losses in aircraft were about equal, with 102 German aircraft destroyed or damaged for the loss of 110 British fighters, although nearly 40 of these were destroyed on the ground. Aircrew losses showed more disparity, with the *Luftwaffe* losing 160 aircrew and the RAF sustaining only 29 casualties.

Operations slackened off in the following week due to pilot fatigue and bad weather and Goering, again supplied with inferior intelligence, abandoned attacks on the radar chain, not realising its huge strategic value and instead, from 24 August, concentrated his attacks on aircraft factories and RAF airfields. The airfield attacks proved costly to the RAF in terms of both men and machines but the addition of some Fleet Air Arm and Commonwealth pilots as well as the well-trained and highly experienced Czech and Polish contingents quickly overcame this shortfall. The Germans were less fortunate and obtaining replacement pilots

was one of their most significant problems as was increasingly poor morale amongst the *Luftwaffe* in general. By 7 September, aircrew casualties and failure to destroy the RAF on the ground led Goering to abandon the airfield attacks and begin the Blitz on London, leaving the RAF stations to recover.

Although there have been disagreements over the extent of the danger this period presented to Fighter Command, modern consensus seems to be that the RAF never really came close to the destruction planned by the *Luftwaffe.* Fighter Command's aircraft actually increased between 3 August and 7 September from 1,769 to 1,906 machines and fighter pilot numbers grew by over 30% between June and August 1940, with approximately 1,400 continually available during August and the first weeks of September. The Germans never had more than 1,200 pilots, a deficiency of up to one-third and according to Richard Overy: 'If Fighter Command were The Few, the German fighter pilots were fewer.'

	Participating aircrew	Dead/wounded/ missing or captured	Aircraft in service	Aircraft destroyed
RAF	5,000	1612/422/0	1,963	1,744
Luftwaffe	7,500	2,585/735/925	2,550	1,977

Fighter Command and Luftwaffe casualties during the Battle of Britain. 1 July-7 September 1940

Total aircrew includes fighters, bombers, reconnaissance and Coastal Command aircraft.

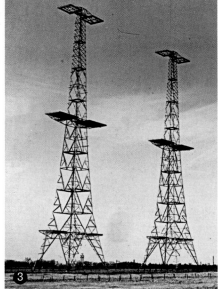

1. Early picture of a Supermarine Spitfire attached to 602 Squadron **2.** RAF Beaufighter MkII, photographed in 1941, when it was the main RAF nightfighter **3.** Chain Home tower, showing the substantial structure which proved difficult for the Luftwaffe to significantly damage

Characteristics	Supermarine Spitfire Mk V B	Hawker Hurricane Mk.IIC	Messerschmitt Bf 109E	Messerschmitt Bf 110 C-4
Maximum speed	370mph	340mph	354mph	348mph
Combat radius	470mi	600mi	411mi	1,500mi
Service ceiling	36,500ft	36,000ft	36,089ft	35,000 ft
Crew	Pilot	Pilot	Pilot	Pilot and observer

Performance characteristics of Battle of Britain fighters

Fighters and tactics

The differences in performance between the Bf 109 and the Spitfire and the Hawker Hurricane MkII were marginal, although the two British fighters were slightly more manoeuvrable. One major disadvantage which both British fighters suffered from was a tendency for the engine to cut out when going into a steep dive because fuel was forced out of the carburettor under the effects of negative-g, something which did not happen to the fuel-injected Bf 109. Both the Spitfire and Hurricane were also poorly armed, the eight Browning .303 machine guns often proving ineffective against German aircraft, trials showing that over 4,500 rounds were required to destroy an enemy machine.

Perhaps the RAF's biggest disadvantage lay in its fighter tactics. Instead of using the open, four finger formation of the Luftwaffe, British senior officers insisted upon tight V-shaped formations based upon three aircraft, which only allowed the leading aircraft any degree of all-round visibility and proved fatally flawed against the more experienced Luftwaffe. Many in the RAF appreciated the limitations of this system but with new pilots now seeing action for the first time, it would have been problematic to attempt to re-train them, although by 1941, a modification of the German system had been adopted. Some tactical changes were introduced as well, in particular the Big Wing concept proposed by Trafford Leigh-Mallory and implemented by Douglas Bader. Keith Parkes, who led 11 Group in the battle and Dowding were against this tactic however, and his opposition to Leigh-Mallory is said to have been what forced Dowding to step down in October 1940.

Specialist operations by the RAF

Specialist operations were also conducted during this period including; the Dambuster's raid by 617 Squadron (Operation *Chastise*) and the raid on Gestapo HQ in Copenhagen, Denmark (Operation *Carthage*). The target of the *Carthage* raid was Gestapo HQ, which was hit and destroyed, although, unfortunately, the raid also mistakenly attacked a nearby Catholic school, resulting in the deaths of 86 schoolchildren and 39 adults.

CASUALTIES OF OPERATIONS CHASTISE AND CARTHAGE

Operation Chastise
Aircraft on operation:
19 Lancasters
Aircraft lost on operation:
8 Lancasters
Aircrew casualties
53 killed

Operation Carthage
Aircraft on operation:
20 Mosquitos, 30 P51 Mustangs
Aircraft lost on operation:
Four Mosquitos and 2 P51
Aircrew casualties
9 aircrew killed

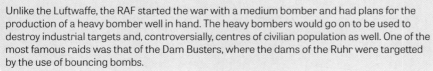

Unlike the Luftwaffe, the RAF started the war with a medium bomber and had plans for the production of a heavy bomber well in hand. The heavy bombers would go on to be used to destroy industrial targets and, controversially, centres of civilian population as well. One of the most famous raids was that of the Dam Busters, where the dams of the Ruhr were targetted by the use of bouncing bombs.

1942-1944: Later strategic bombing and the changing role of fighters

With the Battle of Britain successfully concluded, the RAF began to deploy its aircraft against German targets in Europe, while at the same time operating contingents in the Middle East and Malta.

Fighter Command began operations in 1941 over North Western France, with the intention of gaining air superiority, although the short range of the Spitfire and the quality of the new Fw190 fighter meant they were relatively unsuccessful. Attacks on the *Luftwaffe's* night bombing raids went well however, and London's Blitz was all but over by 10 May 1941, when Hitler withdrew the *Luftwaffe to* begin preparations for Operation *Barbossa*, the invasion of Soviet Russia. Fighter operations between 1942 and 1944 also included air cover for the Dieppe raid and after the autumn of 1942, protection for the USAAF's daylight bombing raids.

Bomber Command also saw a number of changes after the end of the Blitz. In September 1941, precision raids on military targets were abandoned in favour of unrestricted area bombing, whose purpose was explained in an extract from a British Air Staff paper of that month: 'The ultimate aim of an attack on a town area is to break the morale of the population which occupies it... The immediate aim, is ... twofold, namely, to produce (i) destruction and (ii) fear of death...'

After the introduction of the Handley-Page Halifax and Avro Lancaster, together with an effective bombsight, raids of this type began with the first attack against Lübeck on 28/29 March 1942 by 234 bombers, which turned the city into an ash heap and continued with 1,000 bomber raids against Cologne (May 1942: 470 killed), Hamburg (July 1943: 42,000 killed), Dresden (February 1945: 25,000 killed) and Berlin (1943-1945: 350,000 killed), as well as a number of other German cities. Harris' justification for such horrendous casualties was simple: 'Attacks on cities are strategically justified in so far as they preserve the lives of Allied soldiers. I do not personally regard the whole of the remaining cities of Germany as worth the bones of one British Grenadier.'

The Heinkel He.111 and Dornier Do.17 medium bombers caused localised damage during the Blitz but could not deliver a big enough payload to disrupt the British arnament industry which was already widely dispersed. The Allied retaliation was severe, with the centres of Hamburg, Dresden and Nuremburg being destroyed with the loss of thousands of civilian lives.

North Africa

In addition to their essential role in Europe, the RAF were also responsible for the conduct of the air war in North Africa and the defence of Malta. The responsibility for the desert campaign fell to RAF Middle East, which was composed of four separate commands: RAF Middle East (for Egypt), RAF Iraq, RAF Mediterranean (at Malta) and RAF Aden. Italy declared war in June 1940 and the new commander, Air Vice Marshal Sir Arthur Longmore, found himself with just 29 squadrons and a total of 300 aircraft.

Prior to the Italian invasion, the RAF in Egypt focused the activities of its nine squadrons on ground support, reconnaissance and short periods of aerial combat with the Regia Aeronautica, utilising a tiny force of Gloster Gladiators, Westland Lysanders and Blenheim bombers. It had some notable successes, particularly against the Italian bombers but it was perfectly obvious that the force was too small and replacement by sea and the Western Mediterranean was too problematic to be feasible, so an alternative route was developed, via the Gold Coast and Khartoum, and, by November 1940, the RAF in Egypt had improved its status with two Wellingtons squadrons and another two of Hurricanes. They began their first air campaign as part of Operation *Compass* (operations against the Italian Army between December 1940-February 1941) but the British Army were moving so fast and hard that, often, supporting aircraft were forced to use an air strip in advance of the Army.

When Afrika Korps operations began in March 1941, their Bf 109 fighters came with them and, for a short interval, gained ascendency over the WDAF (Western Desert Air Force: renamed October 1940). Although the WDAF always had to utilise less-modern types of aircraft, like the P-40 Tomahawks/Kittyhawks, they always outnumbered their Axis opponents and were able to provide support for the 8th Army, although the WDAF losses were excessively heavy. However, in 1942, the DAF reorganised its tactics and began to receive more modern aircraft, Spitfires being introduced in August 1942 to establish air superiority, which allowed the WDAF to begin to eradicate the Bf 109s. WDAF

units also adopted the *Luftwaffe* concept of tactical air support by controlling fighter-bombers via radio, as well as improving on this technique by introducing cab ranks of fighter-bombers in the air and waiting to attack specific tactical targets. These techniques provided vital air support to the Eighth Army until the end of the war and were subsequently adopted with even greater success during *Overlord*.

Malta

Malta was a strategically important island in in the Mediterranean, being the only Allied base between Gibraltar and Alexandria. Rommel recognised its importance early in his Western Desert Campaign and between June and December 1940 the Italians tried to bomb the island into submission, opposed only by some obsolete RAF Gloster Gladiators. The Gladiators and AA guns took a heavy toll however, and circumstances were such that the British began to reinforce the island from October 1940, with Wellingtons, Hurricanes and other modern aircraft.

British naval success at Taranto seemed to indicate the Italians were almost beaten.

The appearance of the *Luftwaffe's Fliegerkorps X* in January 1941 gave the RAF considerable trouble in maintaining aircraft numbers and the importation of spare parts. However, despite some considerable success during January-April 1941, German participation in the battle for Malta terminated with the beginning of *Barbossa*, the German invasion of Russia. The RAF and Royal Navy quickly re-established dominance in the area and the Royal Navy set about destroying Rommel's supply links. By December 1941, the *Luftwaffe* were back, although the introduction of Spitfires between March and June 1942 quickly destroyed the *Luftwaffe* squadrons and by the end of May 1942, *Luftwaffe* forces had been reduced to just 83 serviceable aircraft compared with the several hundred available two months earlier.

Supplies were running short though and it was only after the ships of the Pedestal convoy fought their way through to Malta in August 1942 that things began to improve. The appointment of Keith Parkes to command in Malta sealed the *Luftwaffe's* fate - Parkes manoeuvrings his aircraft so that daylight raids by the Axis amounted to suicide. The British were once again attacking Axis supply routes, although still being bombed daily by the *Luftwaffe*, and during 1942 deprived Rommel of half his supplies and two thirds of his fuel oil. By November 1942 the seige of Malta was over.

Service	Original numbers of aircraft	Aircraft losses	Aircrew losses
RAF	716 fighters and bombers	43 fighters	2,301 killed and wounded
Luftwaffe and Regia Aeronautica	2,000+ fighters and bombers	532 fighters and bombers	17,240 killed

RAF casualties during the Siege of Malta

④

D-Day

The early role of the RAF in Operation *Overload* was one of supply and disruption. Arms drops to resistance groups were followed by attacks on road and rail links, as well as the destruction of airfields, attacks all meant to convince the German DKW that the invasion was intended for the Calais/ Dieppe region. Closer to 6 June, RAF fighters flew air patrols to isolate the landing beaches from German fighter attack while Bomber Command superintended the delivery of parachute and glider troops. The also flew sorties against V-1 sites, while continuing the area bombing campaign and providing support for ground troops. As the Allies moved forward the fighters continued their cover role but also began to operate in support of the ground troops, using Hawker Tempests and Typhoons as tank-busters.

April 1945 saw the end of WWII and many RAF personnel found themselves out of the only job they had ever known and sent back to civilian life. For these men, sick of fighting, it became their job to start again, this time in an attempt to win the peace.

Perspectives

The RAF's most significant attribute during WWII was the ability to learn quickly and adapt to the new technologies appearing with such relentless speed. Time and again, during the Battle of Britain, the Battle for Malta, the area bombing raids and the Wafer's operations, RAF aircrews demonstrated an intellectual and physical adaptability which was at least equal to that of the *Luftwaffe*. Add to this the notoriously poor leadership shown by many of the senior German figures in the air force, men for the most part elected to command because of the quality of their National Socialist credentials, rather than any ability to lead a highly intelligent and skilful group of men like the *Luftwaffe's* pilots and perhaps the end result was inevitable. Certainly, if Goering had received better support from *Luftwaffe* Intelligence and had continued bombing RAF bases during 1941 as a result, in addition to having the necessary strength of mind to ignore Hitler and adhere to a single fixed strategic objective, the outcome of WWII might have been very different.

1. A Kittyhawk of the Western Defence Force was a match for Italian aircraft but not the planes of the Luftwaffe. **2.** The antiquate Gloster Gladiator was used for recon in North Africa. **3.** Centres of civilian population were a controversial target. **4.** A Supermarine Spitfire in the livery of the planes flying during the D-Day invasion

RAF AIRCREW CASUALTIES BETWEEN 1939 AND 1945

Total aircrew serving in the RAF
180,000
Fighter Command casualties:
3,690 killed, 1,215 wounded and 601 captured.
Bomber Command casualties:
55,573 killed, 8,403 wounded and 9,838 captured, out of a total of 125,000 aircrew.
Coastal Command casualties:
8,218 killed and 2086 wounded. Few Coastal Command aircrew were captured as their operations were confined to British sea areas.

The CANTERBURY
AUCTION Galleries

AUCTIONEERS AND
VALUERS OF FINE ART
ANTIQUES AND
COLLECTORS' ITEMS

WE ARE ACTIVELY SEEKING COLLECTIONS FOR OUR
2018 SALES CALENDAR

Commission Paid for Successful Introductions

CANTERBURY (01227) 763337   www.thecanterburyauctiongalleries.com

THE COLD WAR YEARS

An iron curtain had fallen across eastern Europe. How was the RAF to respond to this new threat?

Words Tim Heath

W ith the end of World War II and defeat of Nazi Germany, a role in which Britain's RAF was pivotal, a new, more worrying, enemy began to emerge. At the war's end Germany was effectively divided into zones of occupation by Britain, America, France and the USSR [Union of Soviet Socialist Republics]. However relations between Russia and the West soon deteriorated. It would have been foolish to think that two such opposing ideologies could have continued as an alliance beyond WWII. America had won the race to develop

the first atomic bomb and had used it successfully twice against the Japanese on 6 and 9 August 1945. These events brought about the surrender of the Japanese and the end to World War II.

There was genuine concern about Soviet aggression in Europe and geopolitical tensions would lead to an era which became known as the Cold War. The Cold War was the stand-off between East and West which lasted until 1991. Tensions rose further when, on 29 August 1949, the Soviets conducted their first successful test of an atomic bomb. Russia was also busy developing long range bomber aircraft

capable of delivering the new weapon. To face the Soviet threat, the North Atlantic Treaties Organization was created to guarantee West Germany, and western Europe, security.

The British Air Ministry, the branch responsible for the design and procurement of new aircraft for the RAF, were, even at this stage, slow in learning lessons which should have become apparent during the latter stages of WWII. The RAF had been equipped with Britain's first operational jet fighter aircraft in the Gloster Meteor from 27 July 1944. The first RAF Squadron to be equipped with this aircraft was

616 Squadron which was based at RAF Doncaster. The Meteor F MKIII was designed as a fighter fitted with four 20-mm Hispano cannon fitted two either side of the front fuselage firing forward. The F MKIII possessed a top speed of around 486mph. This was not very inspiring performance considering that there were still piston engine fighter aircraft still in service with the RAF that could almost match it. It appeared the Germans had a much better understanding of the design requirements for jet powered fighter aircraft. In the excellent Messerschmitt Me262, Messerschmitt Me163B Komet jet and rocket powered fighters of WWII the Germans had utilised swept-wing concepts in both aircraft. Both these German fighters were potentially war-winning aircraft and it is a mystery as to why the post-war Allies failed to capitalise on their revolutionary design concepts.

The Meteor was a good aircraft but with its straight wing plan it was merely a piston engine design fitted with jet engines. However, the Meteor served the RAF well during the early Cold War era where it was modified and used in many roles including that of two seater trainer and two seat night fighter. The night fighter version had a stretched nose design containing the radar for night interception. The radar was operated by a second crew member seated behind the pilot. Other jet fighter designs soon came into service including the de Havilland Venom. Again the design of the venom centred around straight wings plus a twin boom tail design. The Venom first flew on 2 September 1949 and operated in the fighter bomber and night fighter roles. The Venom, like the Meteor, was armed with four 20-mm cannon but could also carry combinations of bombs and rockets for the ground attack role. The Venom also saw action during the Suez Crisis, the Malayan Emergency and the Aden Emergency where it proved very popular with pilots.

The first RAF Squadron to operate the Venom was No.11 Squadron, one of the oldest RAF Squadrons, based at Coningsby.

The de Havilland Vampire was another aircraft identical to the Venom which saw service from 1946. RAF Squadrons of the Second Tactical Air Force based in West Germany operated the Venom which replaced wartime fighters such as the Hawker Typhoon, Tempest and P51 Mustang. The Vampire had a top speed of 548mph and was armed with four 20mm Hispano canon and could carry 907kg of bombs or rockets. It was clear these early, post-war jet aircraft, optimised for the fighter role, were just an interim measure. It is very unlikely any of them would have been much of a match in air-to-air combat with aircraft such as the Soviet Mig-15.

The Folland Gnat XM691 was originally used by the Red Arrows before being replaced by the BAe Hawk

The de Havilland Venom was quickly replaced in the early 1950s but saw combat in the Suez crisis and was a popular export

A brace of Gloster Meteor IIIs. Although jet powered, the design was very much from the piston-engine era

Another interim design was the Hawker Hunter jet fighter which entered RAF service in 1954. The Hunter was a swept wing, single-jet engine, sub-sonic design, armed with four 30mm Aden cannon. It could also carry various combinations of rockets and bombs. The Hunter served in RAF Squadrons all over the world including India, Aden and Germany. Although popular with pilots the Hunter did experience some serious technical issues early on. One such problem was associated with the tailplane actuator. This was certainly the case in the loss of Hawker Hunter XG236 whose pilot, Flying Officer Brian Walter Schooling, died when the tailplane actuator failed during a dive over the Kielder Reservoir area on 14 February 1958. F/O Schooling, whilst initially blamed for the accident, later had his name cleared by aviation historian and researcher Mr Jim Corbett of the NEEACR.

Other pilots expressed reservations over the Hunter with regard to its suitability as a fighter when compared to Soviet designs of that era. Many RAF pilots were also of the opinion the Hunter could be an unforgiving aircraft. Either way the Hunter was a common sight in the skies over the UK, well into the late 1970s.

The main role proposed for the early RAF jet fighter aircraft was that of interception of Russian bomber aircraft. It soon became apparent that the RAF of the Cold War needed a leap in technology both in fighter and nuclear-capable bomber designs. Although slow in coming off the drawing board, perhaps one of the finest British fighter aircraft ever to have been designed, post-WWII, was that of the supersonic English Electric Lightning. This was a single seat jet fighter which first flew on 4 August 1954. The Lightning was a radical departure from the mundane designs of the early post-WWII years. It featured a swept wing design, two Rolls Royce Avon Turbojet engines and a harder-hitting 30mm Aden cannon armament. The cannon were fitted in pairs, either in the ventral [belly] position or top of the forward fuselage, the

The Gloster Javelin served until the mid-1960s as an all-weather interceptor, despite being sub-sonic

616 Squadron was issued with the relatively slow Meteor, at RAF Manston in Kent

The Hunter served in RAF Squadrons all over the world including India, Aden and Germany

A Hawker Hunter on display at the Yorkshire Air Museum near York

gun ports either side, just forward of the cockpit. The Lightning could carry various combinations of air to ground rockets for the ground attack role and its performance was staggering in comparison to anything else the RAF had previously in service. With a top speed of 1,300mph, able to carry a new generation of air-to-air missiles specially developed for the air interception role, the Lightning proved the nemesis to any Russian bomber straying too close to NATO airspace. The first RAF Squadron to

be equipped with this superb fighter aircraft was No.74 Squadron.

The Lightning has been described by many pilots as like being strapped to a missile. Ex-RAF pilot Flying Officer Norman Green was asked what the Lightning was like to fly and he replied, candidly, "It's f******g fast as f**k, simply unbelievable performance. You haven't truly flown unless you've flown a Lightning!"

The Gloster Javelin was another fighter aircraft which entered service in the mid 1950s. The Javelin was an aesthetically pleasing aircraft in appearance. Its twin Armstrong Siddeley Sapphire 7R turbojet engines, T-tail design, coupled with large delta wing configuration, made it, as one pilot remarked, "One of those aircraft you just had to fly."

The primary role of the Javelin was night fighter and all weather fighter/interceptor. It carried a heavy armament of four 30mm Aden cannon, arranged two in each wing, plus options for up to four de Havilland Firestreak, passive infra red, air-to-air missiles. The only drawback with the Javelin was its performance. It was subsonic, possessing a top speed of 710mph. Clearly there was still much room for improvement. As the threat of a superpower nuclear confrontation steadily grew throughout the 1950s the RAF's requirement for nuclear-capable bombers to form a strategic nuclear strike force was essential. The result was the V-Force or Bomber Command Main Force.

The first of the nuclear capable bombers to equip the V-Force Squadrons was the Vickers Valiant which first flew in 1951 and

An English Electric Lightning at the International Air Tattoo, held at RAF Boscombe Down

entered service in 1955. The enigmatic Avro Vulcan followed with its first flight in 1952 entering service in 1956 and the Handley Page Victor which also had its first flight in 1952 entering service in 1958.The Valiants were soon withdrawn from RAF service due to fatigue issues in their wing structures.

RAF tactics also had to evolve along with the new V-Force bombers. It was soon discovered that the Soviet S-75 Dvina surface-to-air missile could easily bring down high altitude aircraft. Soviet territory bristled with missile defences; the only way for a bomber to be sure of getting through to make a successful nuclear strike was at low level. The V-Force bombers did not possess supersonic performance and the Vulcan was the fastest with its maximum speed of 645mph.

The V-Force bombers were formed into squadrons that would be on 24 hour readiness, seven days a week, 360 weeks of the year. The aircraft were well dispersed to outlying airfields to prevent the enemy from disabling the force in a single strike. This also helped with the rapid reaction during an alert as there would be no queues of

The Soviet S-75 Dvina surface to air missile could easily bring down high altitude aircraft

aircraft waiting to take off. At the sound of the alert crews were required to be airborne in the minimum time possible. They were often billeted in caravans near to the aircraft. "Usually a 15 yard sprint," as one V-Force Vulcan crewman remarked. Flying Officer Keith Markley Ratray once revealed in an interview, "The V-Force bombers had a white anti-nuclear flash paint scheme in the early days. The Bombers themselves looked big from the outside but inside we were cramped like sardines. There were no defensive measures such as machine guns

or cannon. To survive, the idea would be to fly into enemy territory at zero altitude and high speed where their radar equipment would struggle to detect us, at least until it was too late. We could have carried conventional atomic or thermo-nuclear bombs into Soviet Russia. On identifying the target you would climb as fast as possible release the weapon and turn for home. More often than not the backwash of the weapon going off would be felt inside the aircraft. I think had we done that we would have still probably been intercepted on the way back home. They may have been suicide missions in most respects. The Blue Steel missile was a little better as it was a stand-off missile. This meant it could be aimed and fired at the target while you were still a long way from it. I still believe, even now, that success would have depended upon the training and exemplary bravery of the RAF aircrews. Thank heavens that we never got a real alert."

The role of medium bombing was catered for by the English Electric Canberra which was also used in the RAF reconnaissance role finally being retired in 2006! By 1961

RAF Lightning intercepts a Russian bomber somewhere over the North Sea during the Cold War

The Buccaneer was originally designed in the 1950s for the Royal Navy carriers

The Hunter broke the world air speed record in 1953 achieving 727.63mph

The Blue steel nuclear missile was part of Britain's nuclear deterrent against Soviet aggression

the Cold War became hot as the Soviets began to erect the hated Berlin Wall. This concrete edifice separated west from east from 1961 to 1989. When the US cancelled the Skybolt air-launched nuclear missile programme it threw the whole RAF V-Force concept into chaos. After much discussion it was decided that the Royal Navy should take over the main nuclear deterrent role while the RAF would then concentrate on a tactical nuclear capability combined with ground attack, fighter/interception and interdiction roles. This certainly gave the RAF a greater area of flexibility and which is why many of the new fighter aircraft coming into service around this time were applied to the above roles. Pilots entering the RAF were expected to learn the rudiments of air-to-air combat with rockets, missiles and guns and also that of ground attack against enemy armoured vehicles, supply areas and emplacements. The RAF was no longer fulfilling a point defence role as warfare was gradually changing and aircraft, along with their pilots, had to change accordingly. America joined the UK having bases situated all across the country and both the RAF and US Air Forces trained together in combined operations and exercises. This gave the West a greater flexibility in addressing the threat posed by the Soviet Union over UK aerospace and indeed in the European theatre. The US air force brought some much needed muscle into the NATO air defence equation.

Perhaps the finest US Cold War fighter bomber design was that of the McDonnell Douglas F-4 Phantom. The Phantom was a twin-engine all weather long range

Venoms of 45 Squadron. It saw action in the Suez Crisis, the Malayan Emergency and the Aden Emergency

supersonic aircraft. The Phantom had a crew of two pilot and weapons/radar officer and possessed a multi-role capability in a supersonic package. It was adopted by the RAF and the Fleet Air Arm of the Royal Navy. The Phantom became the principal combat aircraft of the 1960s and was still in limited service with the RAF in the 1990s. The pilots of the RAF loved the Phantom as it was fast, it could fight and bomb, and hold its own against anything in the Soviet inventory. It could carry an array of weapons on underwing and centreline stores including rockets, missiles, bombs and 20mm gun packs. The Phantom could also carry the B28, B43 and B57 tactical nuclear weapons. RAF Flying Officer Ratray said of the Phantom, "We could probably have wiped out a good proportion of the Soviet Union with a good Squadron of Phantoms carrying tactical nuclear weapons. The Phantom was immensely fast at 1,386mph and you could really get down and hug the ground with it. I loved it and it was one of the best aircraft I have ever flown. In the event of war with the Soviets its role would have been to knock down the Soviet bombers over the sea before they could arrive over the UK with their nuclear payloads. Of all the aircraft I feel the Phantom and, of course, the Lightning, could have achieved this admirably."

It would be some years before true multi-role combat aircraft would be equipping RAF squadrons. That said, many remarkable designs began to appear off the drawing boards. Aircraft such as the Folland Gnat initially designed as a sub-sonic fighter yet became one of the RAF's primary trainer aircraft; the Hawker Harrier with its VSTOL vectored thrust design considered an aviation breakthrough, the Anglo-French SEPECAT Jaguar strike fighter.

It still seemed that while the quality of the RAF aircrew during the Cold War period was never questioned, aircraft design was slow to react to the changing world.

This changed to a degree with the development of the Panavia Tornado the RAF's first true MRCA or Multi Role Combat Aircraft. The Tornado was a twin-engined, variable geometry, swing-wing aircraft bringing a true multi-role capability to RAF Squadrons. Tornado was, in essence, a development of Cold War paranoia. Designed to carry nuclear weapons deep into the heart of the Soviet Union at low-level supersonic speed guided by a suite of complex avionics. Tornado's performance of 2,490mph, two man crew and impressive weapons load, which included nuclear weapons, gave the RAF something it had been lacking for years. Both bomber and fighter variants would emerge from the

The Vulcan heavy bomber was designed to deliver a nuclear payload but was to see service in the Falklands Conflict

multi-nation consortium of the UK, West Germany and Italy.

The UK had foolishly scrapped its large Naval aircraft carriers capable of distributing whole Squadrons of supersonic fighter aircraft, such as the Phantom, to wherever it would be needed, in favour of the mini aircraft carrier which, at best, could carry a few helicopters. Luckily the RAF had the Hawker Harrier in service with the Fleet Air Arm when Argentina invaded the Falklands Islands in1982. Although designed for Soviet aggression in Europe, it turned out to be the Harrier's finest hour, even though Cold-War Britain had failed to heed the lessons of the past.

Fur Lined Leather
Flying Jacket

Sizes Small - 3XL
£99

Order Online at
www.meanandgreen.com
or call 01902 423868

Children's sizes also available £75

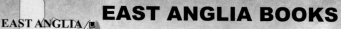

EAST ANGLIA BOOKS

Aviation and Military Books for the
Historian – Collector – Enthusiast

Extensive range of USAAF, RAF and other Air Force histories,
operations, personal stories, airfields, individual aircraft types, wrecks
& relics, nose art, aviation art, camouflage & markings, land warfare &
vehicles, modelling, manufacturers and much more plus a large range of
second-hand.

Wartime Jeeps: Includes 11 prototypes and variants. Hdbk, 200 colour
illustrations, 120pp. **£25.00**
Luftwaffe Crash Archive Volume 11: Series by Nigel Parker. A4 size
softback, approx' 130pp, well illustrated throughout. **£25.00**
Suppliers of the Grey Wolves: Axel Urbanke. German/English text plus
CD, 336pp. 305 photos including 5 in colour, 33 clr maps. **£59.00**
Invasion Airfields Then & Now: After The Battle. By Winston Ramsey,
After The Battle. Hdbk, 225pp, fully illustrated. **£34.95**
All Along The Control Tower V3: Hdbk, high quality photos of remaining
control towers. Vols 1 and 2 currently available. **£39.95**
Fortresses Over Deenethorpe: Story of the 401st BG. By C Bishop/M
Osborn. Hdbk, photos, charts, tables, MIA crew reports, daily diary **£40.00**
A Battle of Britain Spitfire Squadron: Men & Machines of 152 Sqdn by
Danny Burt. Hdbk, 256pp, illustrated **£25.00**
British Secret Projects 2: Jet Bombers Since 1949. By Tony Butler.
Hdbk, 288pp over 350 photos & drawings. **£27.50**
Wings of the Black Cross Special No 2: Junkers Ju 87. By Mark
Proulx. Laminated cover, 48pp, illustrated. **£24.95**

Our new 2018 catalogue is now available! Please contact us for
a free copy!

All our books are packed carefully by hand!

PO Box 12408, Stansted, Essex, CM24 8UZ, England
Telephone 01279-813791 / Email sales@eastangliabooks.com
Website www.eastangliabooks.com
Facebook www.facebook.com/eastangliabooks

LINCOLNSHIRE AVIATION
HERITAGE CENTRE

East Kirkby Airfield, Nr Spilsby
Lincolnshire PE23 4DE
Tel: 01790 763207
Email: enquiries@lincsaviation.co.uk

- **AWARD WINNING DISPLAYS**
- **FLYING DISPLAYS THROUGHOUT THE YEAR**
- **RE-ENACTMENT EVENTS**
- **THE PERSONAL STORIES OF BOMBER COMMAND**

Home to AVRO Lancaster NX611 'Just Jane'
Dakota N473DC & Mosquito HJ711

THE 'LANCASTER' AIRCRAFT
AVRO TYPE '683' Mk. I. & III.
FLIGHT ENGINEER'S NOTES
FOR 'LANCASTER'
AIRCRAFT

. Bomber Command Museum
set up on a Lancaster Bomber
airfield

. Experience the sights, sounds,
smells & atmosphere of a
Bomber Command airfield

. **The only place in Europe
where you can ride in a
Lancaster**

. Biggest Bomber Command
museum in the world

www.lincsaviation.co.uk

FIGHTING THE FALKLANDS

It was the biggest challenge since the end of WWII – how to retake a set of islands in the South Atlantic, thousands of miles away

Words Martin Taylor

D uring the Falklands Conflict the RAF had to re-write the manual and proved achieving victory required flexibility, quick thinking and effective planning. These were as important a weapon as the aircraft. The role of the RAF in the conflict was epitomised by the Black Buck Vulcan bomber missions and the RAF Harrier actions against ground targets on the islands. However, the vital part the RAF played in transport and logistics should not be overlooked as this enabled the final goal of retaking the islands from Argentine

forces by ground troops.

In 1982 the RAF was winding down the remaining V Force bombers and was prepared to fight a NATO-led campaign against the Soviet Union in Europe as part of its Cold War commitments. Suddenly, a requirement to deploy aircraft arrived, with the Argentine invasion, that was way beyond anything that had been asked before. Just getting the required assets to the conflict zone was a major challenge that required speedy modifications to outdated airframes and out of the box thinking on existing doctrine. For example in the case

of the Black Buck raids beginning on 9 April, a 24 hour engineering effort began to make the raids a reality. Aircraft based at Waddington had to be overhauled and required in-flight refuelling probes sourced from such places as Catterick, Woodford, Goose Bay in Labrador and Wright-Patterson Air Force Base in Ohio. The Vulcan's internal refuelling systems were essentially refitted and the engines tuned. Bomb bays and crew stations also had to be modified to allow for the carriage and delivery of conventional bombs. It took only five days for the necessary modifications to

1. XM607 Pictured in retirement at RAF Waddington (RHL Images) **2.** Handley Page Victor K.2 with refuelling drogues extended (RuthAS) **3.** Aerial reconnaissance photo of Port Stanley Airport. The craters from Black Buck One's bombs are visible in the middle. Black Buck Two's craters are visible more clearly to the left **4.** An AGM-45 Shrike anti-radiation missile as fired in the Black Buck raids (Scott Stewart USAF) **5.** XZ989 Lost power on landing at Port San Carlos airstrip and was the last loss of the conflict **6.** The current day wreckage of one of the Chinooks lost in the conflict today

be completed.

Hercules and VC10 transports flew over 500 missions from the UK to Ascension and transported 5000 personnel and 6000 tonnes of equipment during the course of the conflict. To provide further capacity additional Boeing 707s were chartered and five ex-RAF Belfast freighters were also returned to service. The Hercules deployment included some lengthened C.3 versions but the main type deployed were the standard length C.1 type coming from a pool of over 50 aircraft of 24, 30, 47 and 70 Squadrons of the Lyneham Transport Wing. 47 and 70 Squadrons concentrated on supplying from Ascension to the Falkland Islands, while 24 and 30 squadrons flew missions between Ascension and the UK. 47 Squadron also included a Special Forces flight which may have also been used for covert operations without any official acknowledgement of its purpose.

In the support role, two Nimrod MR1 maritime patrol aircraft were deployed in May from Ascension Island to patrol the area around the Falklands and provide communications with Royal Navy nuclear submarines. A month later, in April, the MR1s were replaced by some of the 13 plus more modern Nimrod MR.2s of 120, 201 and 206 Squadrons based at RAF Kinloss.

RAF Nimrods played a vital role in coordinating aerial refuelling for Victor, Vulcan and Harrier flights throughout the conflict and flew ahead of the task force in the reconnaissance role. By the conclusion of the conflict some Nimrods had been fitted with sidewinder missiles for defence and had been re-equipped to enable air-to-air refuelling.

None of the famous RAF missions flown during the conflict would have been possible without the 20 Victor K.2 tankers of 55 and 57 Squadrons of RAF Marham based at Ascension Island. The Victors initially flew three maritime radar reconnaissance missions which lead up to the recapture of South Georgia. Then, in approximately 600 refuelling sorties, the Victors provided support for other aircraft in often complex

1. An AN/TPS-43 radar set of the same type as targeted in the later Black buck raids **2.** A Hercules C130K and VC10, from 1312 Flight, Mount Pleasant airfield, practice air-to-air refuelling in the skies above the Falkland Islands (Cpl Heidi Cox, RAF) **3.** Members of the General Engineering Firm and flight crew in front of XM607 at RAF Wadding prior to departure for the Falklands following emergency refit (Kazsta10) **4.** A Royal Air Force Harrier GR.3 hovers with its landing gear down – here seen in 1984 **5.** An RAF helicopter crewman pictured flying above Ascension Island during the conflict. Note the popular RAF moustache style of the time (Ken Griffiths)

refuelling patterns. These missions included refuelling fighters staging to Ascension, Hercules long-range supply drops, extending Nimrod maritime patrols and the Vulcan Black Buck raids. RAF Victors also provided air cover as the Atlantic Conveyor transport proceeded to the islands loaded with RAF Harriers and helicopters.

In total four RAF Chinook HC.1 helicopters were despatched on the Atlantic conveyor transport ship and three of these were destroyed when the ship was hit by an Exocet missile launched from an argentine Super Étendard fighter on 25 May. Fortunately one Chinook HC.1 (ZA718/BN) was in the air when the missile struck but the remaining three RAF Chinooks along with all spares and maintenance equipment were totally destroyed in the attack. Prior to the loss of the Chinooks it had been planned that they would aid the ground advance of British troops following landfall on the islands. Though, with only the single Chinook, operational heavy equipment transport was given top priority with the majority of the troops having to walk up to 50 miles before the fighting began in the famous yomp across the Falklands.

RAF Harriers in the conflict

In total, 14 RAF GR.3 aircraft from No.1 (F) squadron were deployed and, although capable of air-to-air combat and armed accordingly, they were used primarily in the ground attack role. This arrangement apparently caused some consternation amongst some deployed RAF pilots who felt they were missing out on an opportunity to engage enemy aircraft. RAF Harrier GR.3s were fitted with sidewinder missiles and ECM pods during the conflict but all aerial engagements were handled by the Navy's Sea Harriers. Also, optional Aden 30mm side mounted gun packs were available for air-to-air and air-to-ground use and were responsible for the destruction of some ground targets. RAF GR.3 aircraft primarily used 1000lb unguided iron bombs and Royal Navy Sneb rocket pods (an unguided air-to-ground 68mm (2.7in) rocket system manufactured by the French company TDA Armaments) to engage ground targets. The Sneb rocket version was selected by the

Royal Navy because of concerns about the safety of RAF rocket systems interacting with the carriers' Naval radar systems.

During the conflict, only four RAF Harrier GR.3s were lost. On 21 May RAF GR.3 XZ972 flown by Flight Lt Jeff Glover crashed after being hit by a Blowpipe missile fired by Argentine Special Forces during an armed reconnaissance mission over Port Howard – fortunately the pilot survived and ejected but was subsequently captured by Argentinian forces. On 27 May RAF GR.3 XZ988 of No. 1 Squadron, piloted by Squadron Leader Bob Iveson, crashed after being hit by small arms fire during an attack on Goose Green. Iveson was able to eject safely and spent three days in hiding before being rescued by British forces.

On 30 May XZ963, piloted by Squadron leader Jerry Pook, attacked Argentine commandos assaulting British forces on Mount Kent and also Port Stanley. During the attacks XZ963's fuel tanks were punctured by small arms fire and

(4)

5

it subsequently ran out of fuel trying to return to HMS Hermes. It ditched into the South Atlantic, 30 miles short of the carrier though Squadron Leader Pook was successfully rescued by the Royal Navy. The final official Harrier casualty of the conflict was on 8 June when RAF GR.3 XZ989 was damaged beyond repair after a loss of power whilst attempting a landing on a metal strip runway at San Carlos Airfield. Wing Commander Pete Squire was flying XZ989 and he walked away from the incident..

RAF Harrier GR.3s destroyed only ground targets during the conflict, however it should be noted that RAF personnel did achieve six air-to-air kills while flying Royal Navy Sea Harriers. Flight Lt David Morgan was one RAF pilot who was attached to the Fleet Air Arm and trained in carrier operations and flew the FRS1 in air combat operations. Previously mentioned, Squadron leader Jerry Pook has also written a comprehensive book detailing all ground attack operations by RAF GR.3 Harriers during the Falklands War. Aircraft destroyed on the ground by GR3s included nine FMA IA 58 Pucará ground attack aircraft, an Agusta A109 helicopter, a Boeing Ch-47C Chinook helicopter, two Aérospatiale Puma SA330L helicopters, four Beechcraft T-34 Mentor ground attack aircraft, two Skyvan 3-M transports and two Bell UH-1H Iroquois helicopters. In addition to this GR.3s destroyed multiple vehicles and installations as well as accounting for a large number of Argentine troop casualties.

Operation Black Buck

Operation Black Buck consisted of seven planned Vulcan raids against Argentine positions on the Falkland Islands, of which five were actually carried out. The most famous was the first attack on the runways at Port Stanley airport on 30 April. On this mission, two Vulcans, XM598 as primary aircraft with XM607 in reserve, were loaded with 21 1,000lb unguided bombs - over nine tons of high explosive. When this was combined with a full fuel load it meant that both aircraft were 2½ tons over their maximum weight. Also, as Ascension Island is a hot environment the Vulcans had to run their engines at 103% power just to get off the ground.

As the Vulcans of Black Buck 1 left Ascension Island and headed towards the Falklands, the requirement for an airborne spare was quickly proven. Squadron Leader John Reeve, of 50 Squadron, reported shortly after take-off that a rubber seal on a side window had failed so the cabin was unable to pressurise. This meant that XM607 had to step into the primary aircraft role with XM598 returning to base. Also, one of the 11 accompanying Victor tankers then had to turn back due to mechanical problems and was also replaced by its airborne spare. On learning of the changes the captain of XM607, Flight Lieutenant Martin Withers, with typical British understatement then announced to his five-man crew, "Looks like we've got a job of work."

FROM THE FALKLANDS CONFLICT TO TODAY

The modern RAF has come a long way since the operation to retake the South Atlantic island

Words Tim Heath

From experiences learned during the 1982 Falklands War it became painfully clear to Britain's RAF that considerable change was necessary, if it were to remain an effective defensive measure not only within Britain's defensive strategy but in the modern world too. The Falklands air war did not exclusively affect the RAF as the Fleet Air Arm bore the brunt of the Falklands air defence commitments. The RAF did, however, bomb the runway at Port Stanley using Vulcan bombers of 44, 50 and 101 Squadrons of the RAF Waddington Wing. The missions were known as Black Buck one to seven. Five of these Black Buck missions were completed. Their effectiveness is still very much debated. However the raids did force the Argentine Air Force to withdraw some of its aircraft from the Stanley airfield but in all disruption was minimal.

There's an argument that the British Naval task force, sent to retake the islands from the Argentine invaders, embarked on the operation with woefully inadequate air defence measures. This was an issue which soon became apparent once the real fighting began upon arrival of the British task force. France had supplied the Argentine air force with the latest Exocet anti-ship missiles. These weapons launched from attacking Argentine aircraft at stand-off distances proved devastatingly effective. The British Naval forces had no counter measure to these new sea skimming missiles. As a result of inadequate defensive measures, Royal Navy ships and crew were lost that should not have been.

So what could the RAF learn from the experiences of the Falklands War, which might aid it in future conflicts? The Panavia Tornado MRCA [Multi Role Combat Aircraft] was in service in 1982 but a lack of adequate airfields meant it could not be deployed in that particular theatre of operations. Had it been it could have proved an effective weapon in bringing the war to an earlier close.

1. Typhoon combat aircraft take off at an airfield in Japan during the Northern Guardian 16 joint exercises Force (RAF/Crown Copyright) **2.** An RAF Tornado being armed prior to a sortie **3.** Eurofighter DA2 on its first flight April 1994

Tornado was the new boy in the RAF armoury at the time. It was by far Britain's most advanced combat aircraft to date. The Tornado was primarily designed to fulfil a variety of operational packages from carrying nuclear weapons into the heart of the Soviet Union, conventional bombing, strike and battlefield interdiction to air interception. It was hoped it would give the RAF an edge over many of its Warsaw Pact rivals of the time. In its original specification it was more a bomber aircraft than a fighter. However its performance, avionics and wide variety of weapons load plus two 27mm Mauser IKWA rapid firing cannon would have surely countered even the slightest of shortcomings. The Tornado had a two man crew of pilot and navigator. The navigator was positioned behind the pilot. The first RAF squadron to operate the Tornado was Number 9 Squadron otherwise known as No.IX(B) Bomber Squadron operating from RAF Marham, Norfolk. Other squadrons which were equipped with the Tornado were Number's 12, 31, 41, 15 (R), 14, 13 and 617 Squadron (The Dam Busters) to name a few. Whilst further new developments in combat aircraft in the RAF were not forthcoming upgrading existing airframes appeared to be the niche. Apart from Tornado there was a multitude of mostly obsolete aircraft in service with Britain's RAF at the time. These included the Sepecat Jaguar, Hawker Siddeley Buccaneer and, of course, the Harrier. Some even argued the case that Tornado itself was obsolete by the mid 1980s.

The US Air Force had aircraft based here in the UK and many British pilots were envious of their US counterparts and the aircraft they had at their disposal. Many RAF pilots of the time felt that the US Air Force was given a blank cheque book for anything it needed. UK Government spending on the RAF, Navy and Army was severely curtailed throughout the 1980s by the Conservative government under Mrs Thatcher. This had a detrimental effect on the UK's ability to defend itself. It meant, more or less, in the event of a major war the UK would not have been able to defend itself in the normal defence context. The Government was of the view that if it all went wrong NATO [North Atlantic Treaties Organisation] would come to our rescue. It can be argued that this policy was influential on Argentina's decision to invade the Falklands Islands. In this climate of defence spending cuts the RAF had little choice but to upgrade their existing airframes with whatever modern equipment's could be allocated them. Britain it would appear

1. Iraqi car destroyed by RAF aircraft 1991 Gulf War **2.** Iraqi tanks destroyed by the RAF in the 1991 Gulf War **3.** Typhoon in Trident Juncture, taking place in Spain and largest NATO exercise since 2002 (RAF/Crown Copyright) **4.** Tornados taking part in Trident Juncture 2015 NATO exercise (RAF/Crown Copyright) **5.** A Tornado and Buccaneer attacking an Iraqi airfield during the 1991 Gulf War **6.** Coalition bomb exploding in the Gulf War

could simply not afford to build her own combat aircraft any longer and were forced into forming consortiums with countries such as Spain, Italy and Germany. This move spread the costs enabling Britain to pursue new aircraft in a much more cost effective fashion. It was in this joint collaboration environment where the Panavia [Pan Aviation] Tornado was conceived.

The RAF, post-Falklands War, became a neglected backwater. The conditions pilots were living in were poor, morale was low and many highly-skilled pilots considered leaving the service. Many could not understand why we were still operating vintage aircraft from the 1950s-1960s. One RAF pilot, who served throughout the 1980s, and wished to remain anonymous, said, "You can only stretch these old aircraft so far. When they reach the end of their service life they should be replaced with something new. We have the Tornado but when I will get chance to go on conversion to that aircraft is anyone's guess. As things stand our aircraft are wearing out and you can only stick new wings and tails on an aircraft for so long before you are playing with pilot's lives. The Vulcans are being phased out and rightly so. We are, though, still flying Hunters, Harriers and Jaguars. Our accommodation is poor, the houses all have rising damp and our wives are all depressed. Not the pretty picture of the dashing fighter pilot of old now is it!"

Resilience has always been one of the great qualities of Britain's RAF pilots. As neglected as they and the military in general were in Britain throughout the mid to late 1980s it appeared things in the world were thankfully quiet. This would all change when Iraq invaded Kuwait on 2 August 1990. This was a worrying development not only for the Middle East but the world too. Forming a coalition of nations which would be largely led by the USA and operating under UN [United Nations] mandate would be no easy task. There would be all manner of political, social and cultural issues to address before western military feet could touch Arab ground. The crews of the RAF had mixed feelings on their deployment to the Arabian Peninsula. Many hoped that the Iraqi President was just sabre rattling and he would withdraw his forces from Kuwait and they'd all be home before Xmas. This was however not to be as Saddam Hussein gambled that the west would not intervene in what many might regard as Arab matters.

As the crisis in the Gulf escalated Britain looked at its options. The bulk of the RAF's commitment to the international coalition formed to remove the Iraqi forces would fall on Tornado. To augment the RAF commitment Sepecat Jaguar, Harrier and Buccaneer aircraft were also marked for deployment to the Gulf. Some of the older aircraft were to operate, not so much in the offensive role, but in what was known as the Wild Weasel role. A Wild Weasel would illuminate surface to air missile threats where they would then be destroyed, typically, with anti-radiation missiles. These weapons launched from a Tornado or other aircraft would home in on the missile's radar system. Tornado itself would be involved in the bombing role if the order was given to go in.

What followed was a steady build-up of troops and their equipment in the Gulf theatre. Hundreds of aircraft of all types were flown in and based in and around Saudi Arabia. Xmas and New Year 1990

4

5

6

passed. It was reminiscent of Britain's Phoney War of 1940. On 17 January 1991 the order to attack targets in Iraq and Kuwait were given. A prolonged bombardment by naval forces stationed off the Gulf and coalition aircraft began. For the RAF and Tornado it would be a blessing of fire. The first bombing raid carried out by the RAF Tornado force reported no casualties and all came back. However the sheer rate of sorties being flown and the volume of anti-aircraft artillery fire they were encountering meant that casualties would be inevitable. The Iraqi forces had SAMs (Surface to Air Missiles) around their airfields and these proved very effective particularly at aircraft operating at low level. The Iraqi airfields were also well defended by multiple anti-aircraft guns of all calibre.

One of the Tornado's which failed to return by the end of that day on 17 January 1991 was the Tornado being flown by Flight Lieutenants Peters and Nichols. They were hit by a SAM during an ultra-low level bombing run against the Ruma airfield in Iraq. Their aircraft, once hit, remained airborne and under control for some minutes before fire forced the crew to eject. They were later captured and paraded on Iraqi television.

Other Tornado crews were not so lucky and a number would be killed as a result of the dense hail of Iraqi anti-aircraft artillery or SAMs. The Tornado crews had the unenviable task of delivering the JP233 sub munition system. The JP233 system scatters anti-runway munitions and area-denial bomblets over a wide area. To deliver this weapon effectively requires an aircraft to fly at a set speed and course for around two miles. This requires exceptional bravery as during the course of a JP233 approach and deployment the pilot cannot take any evasive action to prevent his aircraft from being hit.

What was it like to fly into a heavily defended Iraqi airfield during those initial stages of the 1991 Gulf War? Flight Lieutenant Peter Hawshaw gives his account: 'I was flying more in the support role to help try and draw the Iraqi defences away from the main attack. I think they were confused by all the noise around them as their fire was somewhat wild and lacked co-ordination. It was pretty intimidating and once they woke up a bit they filled the sky with so much rapid cannon fire that you just felt, f*****g hell there is no possibility of us flying through this shit without taking damage. I actually thought at one point we are going to get shot up to shit and either get killed in the aircraft or by those bastards on the ground if they captured us. We were among the lucky ones. I think the only damage on our aircraft was a small hole made by a 14.5mm heavy machine gun round. Overall, Tornado was fragile - it could not take much punishment and was easy to shoot down with anti-aircraft artillery at low level. I think concerns were expressed about the vulnerability of the Tornado operators. All low-level Tornado

1. The RAF Tornado had to fly very dangerous low-level missions in the Gulf War **2.** Tornado getting ready for action overnight for a sortie into Iraq (Crown Copyright) **3.** Members of II (AC) Squadron from the RAF start their participation in Northern Guardian alongside members of 3 Air Wing Japan Air Self Defence Force (RAF/Crown Copyright)

operations were cancelled in favour of higher altitude missions which improved the chances of a crew getting home. Had we carried on as we were we could have slowly lost every Tornado. Anyway we won and we should be proud of that fact and of the Tornado. It coped in a very difficult environment, perhaps a little different to that which it had been designed for.'

As the 1991 Gulf War came to its conclusion with the near annihilation of Iraqi forces fleeing Kuwait along the main Basra Road, the world could breathe a sigh of relief. No nuclear weapons had been used and thousands and thousands of casualties predicted by some had not occurred. No sooner had Saddam Hussein's forces been driven from Kuwait that war clouds were once again gathering in Europe.

When a brutal civil war broke out in the former Yugoslavia multi-national troops were deployed from all over the world under the UNHCR [United Nations High Commissioner for Refugees]. The strategy was simple the UN troops would attempt to provide food, water and various other aid to those cut off or displaced by the fighting. Bosnia in particular came to represent this war which was largely created by Serbian Nationalist aggression in the region where Serbs were the majority of the population. The Bosnian crisis worsened to the point where the UN [United Nations] lost face and respect on the world stage. The RAF provided medical staff and air transportation support for the British UN

troops on the ground. The Tornado F3 ADV [Air Defence Variant] contributed to Operation Deny flight launched in 1993. This was a NATO operation to restrict airspace movements over Bosnia and Herzegovina. In this role the Tornado F3 variant performed admirably. The civil war in the former Yugoslavia would later be concluded but only after Nato intervention.

It was also in 1993 another multi-nation project was emerging between Britain, Germany, Italy and Spain. This project would result in an aircraft regarded as one of the most technologically advanced fighter aircraft in the world. The Eurofighter Typhoon, a single seat fighter aircraft which is now in squadron service with the RAF, suffered delays and setbacks during its developmental process. It was not an easy or cheap aircraft to produce. Typhoon utilises a canard delta configuration, state-of-the-art avionics and can carry a wide range of weaponry from missiles, bombs and rockets.

It is also fitted with an internal 27-mm Mauser rapid firing cannon. Eurofighter Typhoon will be capable of defending Britain's skies for many years.

The UK project test pilot Chris Yeo was elated after his first flight in DA2 [Development Aircraft 2] on 4 April 1994. Chris flew the aircraft out of Wharton, in what had been a greatly anticipated flight for him personally. He commented: "Even at this early stage of its development one can see what an excellent aircraft this is going to be. A true fighter pilots' aircraft."

The RAF has recently taken part in a number of joint training exercises with other air forces, including Trident Juncture in Spain, which was the biggest NATO exercise since 2002, and Northern Guardian, with the Japanese Air Self Defence Force.

With the current world situation, conflict and war can happen at any time. The men of the RAF will continue to be there to make sure the skies over the UK remain safe.

The Armourer

Incorporating *Classic Arms & Militaria*

Monthly magazine encompassing ALL aspects of military history and collecting of militaria

Download the FREE sample issue today

or purchase back issues for just 99p before 31/01/2018

Visit www.pocketmags.com/armourer

HUGH TRENCHARD

Tactless and overbearing, but fondly remembered as the Father of the Royal Air Force

Hugh Montague Trenchard was a native of Somerset, being born in 1873 at Windsor Lodge, Haines Hill in Taunton. He was the son of Henry Trenchard, a solicitor, and Georgina Tower, the daughter of a Royal Navy captain. Seeking a career in the military, Trenchard found himself rejected by both Dartmouth and Woolwich, since he struggled to pass the necessary exams. Nevertheless, he persevered and managed to gain a commission, in 1893, in the Royal Scots Fusiliers.

Joining his regiment in India, Trenchard did not prove popular with fellow officers, earning the nickname 'the Camel' on account of the fact he did not drink and was inarticulate, not to mention socially awkward. However, respect for him grew as

he demonstrated his considerable talents for playing polo – it is said he vigorously fended off a young Winston Churchill during one match – and seemingly had an ability to pick winning horses.

Active service came in late 1899, when Trenchard was sent to South Africa during the Anglo-Boer War. In 1900, he was promoted to Captain and was given the task of forming and training a mounted company. In action, Trenchard proved to be a fine guerrilla leader, but he would be wounded in a Boer ambush and invalided home to England. Yet, despite a serious injury to his left lung, he recovered and returned to South Africa in 1901, demonstrating fearlessness in battle.

Following the defeat of the Boers, Trenchard rose to the rank of Lieutenant-Colonel and undertook a number of

overseas appointments and military related projects. However, in 1910 he fell seriously ill and was again invalided back to England, eventually re-joining the Royal Scots Fusiliers at the reduced rank of Major in 1912. It would be in this year, while looking for new opportunities, that he made the decision to join the newly formed Royal Flying Corps (RFC).

Spending £75 on lessons, Trenchard gained his flying certificate from the Royal Aero Club in July, after a mere 64 minutes in the air. He then went to the Central Flying School in Upavon, Wiltshire, where he was appointed to the staff and became Assistant Commandant, holding the rank of Lieutenant-Colonel. Here, he displayed a talent as an effective organiser and earned the nickname 'Boom', due to his booming manner of speech.

With the outbreak of World War I, Trenchard took command at Farnborough, Hampshire. He slowly began to build up the fledgling RFC, and he even went to the front as an operational commander. From 1915 onwards, Trenchard pushed hard for the development of aircraft and the production of increasing numbers. He wanted more powerful engines, greater armament, cameras, wireless sets and the ability to drop ever bigger bombs. Trenchard also demanded constant aggression from his pilots and observers while in the air.

During this time, Trenchard began to develop a doctrine: He believed that persistent aerial attacks were needed to achieve air supremacy, which in turn would permit devastating air attacks on the enemy's industrial centres and vital lines of communication to the front. However, he did not believe aircraft should be used as a defence against aircraft and he was opposed to the issue of parachutes, since he believed they undermined fighting aggression.

In August 1915, Trenchard was appointed head of the RFC in France, and promoted to Brigadier-General. However, as the war progressed the casualties suffered by the RFC remained substantially higher than those of the Germans, mainly due to Trenchard's policy of constantly taking the fight to the enemy.

Competition between the RFC and the Royal Naval Air Service (RNAS) for training facilities, aircraft development and production led to both arms being weaker than they should have been. This in turn led to calls for a united service, especially since neither produced an adequate defence against German daylight bombing raids. Thus, on 1 April 1918, the two were merged to form the Royal Air Force, of which Trenchard would be the first head.

Following the end of World War I, the RAF was greatly reduced in size as peace returned. Nevertheless, Trenchard founded an apprentice school at Halton in Buckinghamshire, to train ground crews, and a cadet college at Cranwell in Lincolnshire, where officers would likewise be trained. He also established a staff college at Andover in Hampshire, for future leaders of the RAF.

At an operational level, Trenchard proved the RAF was well adapted for air policing across the empire, being an effective yet

1. Trenchard (seated third from right) at the Central Flying School, 1913 2. The statue of Hugh Trenchard, Father of the RAF, sits on the Embankment in London 3. Queen Mary and Hugh Trenchard inspect fighter aircraft during World War I 4. Trenchard inspecting cadets at the RAF college for officer training at Caldwell, Lincolnshire 5. Trenchard in conversation with Sir Arthur Tedder during World War II

relatively inexpensive means of doing so. This so-called control without occupation was successful, but it led to failure to prepare for confronting an enemy with the same technological level of advancement as Britain. A fact that would not be properly addressed until 1939, when war with Germany once again loomed.

Trenchard retired from the RAF in 1930, taking up the position of Metropolitan Police Commissioner the following year, a post he held until 1935. With the outbreak of World War II, Trenchard spent time visiting RAF units and championed the service in the House of Lords and the press. However, he never gained the pivotal role he would have liked.

On 10 February 1956, he died, aged 83, but is forever remembered as the Father of the Royal Air Force.

EDWARD 'MICK' MANNOCK

The highest scoring British ace of the Great War and an early pioneer of organised aerial tactics left school at 14

Edward Mannock was not the average World War I pilot. He came from a working-class family, left school at 14 and was an ardent socialist. The 27 year old experienced his first challenge of the war whilst working in Istanbul as a telephone engineer. Turkey supported the Central Powers, and interned Mannock. He was malnourished and became a nuisance to the guards, stealing food and crafting an escape tunnel. As a result, he was locked in a concrete cell. Near death, his fortune turned when he was released back to England under the ironic belief that he was too ill to resume combat operations.

Upon returning to England he made a remarkable recovery, and joined the Royal Army Medical Corps. Mannock was inspired by the stories of the British ace Albert Ball and transferred to the Royal Flying Corps, as he did not like the prospect of spending the war in the Medical Corps. He joined at the age of 29, almost ten years older than most of the other pilots. Mannock was assigned to No. 40 Squadron in the April of 1917, Bloody April as it was known. It was a time when the RFC was losing pilots at such a rate that the Western Front was littered with downed aircraft and the life expectancy for an RFC pilot was eleven days. On top of this grim reality, he was not popular

The life expectancy for an RFC pilot was just eleven days

with his fellow flyers. On his first day at the squadron he sat in the favourite chair of a pilot who was killed that day, and brashly made comments about the way the war was being fought and his theories on air fighting. His first experience of combat did not help matters. On 13 April he flew over no-man's land for the first time and was subjected to a barrage of flak. The shock of this, combined with a dose of inexperience, made him drop out of formation. However, on 19 April 19 he practised attacking a ground target and the right lower wing of his aircraft tore off. Using a large amount of skill, Mannock managed to crash land his aircraft in a field without any fatal consequences. Despite demonstrating his flying skill, he remained largely unpopular.

Mannock's first victory was to come on 7 May when he destroyed a German observation balloon, one of the most dangerous targets to engage. His success slowly continued, downing an Albatros

1

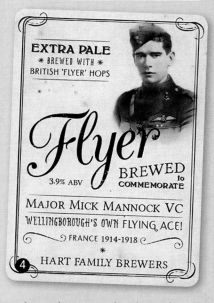

1. A portrait of Mannock in the thick jacket and gloves necessary for flying an open cockpit aircraft **2.** An example of an S.E.5a flying at Old Warden. Mannock flew the S.E.5a from the November of 1917 **3.** A shot of Mannock with his dog **4.** Even in WWI, popular and notable figures were used in advertising

D.III on 7 June. Although his confidence in the air grew, this was not reflected in his personal feelings. His third victory, a DFW CV, crashed behind friendly lines and he rushed by car to view its wreckage. The sight of the mangled plane and inhabitants, along with the dead black terrier mascot in the rear seat made Mannock remark that he, "felt exactly like a murderer." Mannock was privately a nervous individual, on whom the strain of combat took its toll. He carried a revolver around with him, not as some pilots thought to take pop-shots at enemy aircraft, but rather to turn on himself in the event of his aircraft catching fire. Despite his mental struggle, outwardly he was excelling, and was awarded the Military Cross on 19 July, with personal congratulations from AOC Hugh Trenchard.

His reputation increased rapidly in the following weeks, with a promotion to Captain and Flight Commander. By the September 1917, he had 15 victories and had become an aggressive and talented fighter. His position within the squadron also allowed him to start putting into practice his theories on air fighting. He taught new pilots the golden rule of , "Always above, seldom on the same level, never underneath". Mannock also believed in the importance of the squadron flying together and fighting together saying, the "days of the lone fighter were past." He believed in only attacking when he had a numerical advantage and a superior position. It was this combined with his incredible deflection shooting that made

him so successful in the air.

His time with 40 Squadron ended on New Year's Day 1918, shooting down a Hannover CL.III in the newly equipped S.E.5a, his first victory in the type. In March 1918, Mannock returned to France with No. 74 Squadron after some time in England, resting and training. Mannock was assigned as Senior Flight Commander and took the newer pilots under his wing. His time commanding A Flight led to a series of aces being made, as well as Mannock doubling his total to 41.

Scoring three victories on 12 May and four on 21 May, his quickly-rising score led him to proclaim, "If I've any luck I think I may beat old Mac [James McCudden]. Then I shall try to oust old Richthofen." His score further increased and at 52 victories he was given command of No. 85 Squadron, replacing Canadian ace Billy Bishop as the commanding officer. In the weeks that followed he scored a further eight victories with 85 squadron, but his mental state became increasingly fragile. This was worsened by the news of James McCudden's death in an accident. On 26 July, while helping Donald Inglis score his first victory, Mannock's aircraft was hit by a barrage of fire from the German lines and his S.E.5a caught fire and crashed. Mannock had broken his own rule and followed the LVG down so he could confirm Inglis' victory. Mannock has no known grave. Whether he burnt to death or managed to turn that pistol on himself we will never know, though a contemporary report from someone in the

British trenches reports him being thrown out of the aircraft when it crashed. Either way, it was a tragic end to Britain's top scoring ace of World War I. A year later he was awarded a posthumous Victoria Cross after serious lobbying from his comrades, and he remains one of the most successful pilots of both the RFC and RAF with 61 confirmed victories.

EXTRA PALE
★ BREWED WITH ★
BRITISH 'FLYER' HOPS

Flyer

BREWED to COMMEMORATE

3.9% ABV

MAJOR MICK MANNOCK VC
WELLINGBOROUGH'S OWN FLYING ACE!
FRANCE 1914-1918
★
HART FAMILY BREWERS

RONALD J MITCHELL

The creator of the Supermarine Spitfire started his career by designing seaplanes before moving on to building record-setting entries in the Schneider Trophy

Mitchell was born in Staffordshire in 1895. He initially began an apprenticeship with Kerr Stuart & Co, a local engineering firm producing locomotives, in 1911, aged 16. After finishing his apprenticeship, he was moved to the drawing office of the firm, while he also studied engineering and mathematics at night school.

In 1917, aged 22, he left Kerr Stuart and found a job with the Supermarine Aviation Works at Southampton. He advanced rapidly through the company, becoming Chief Engineer in 1920 and Technical Director in 1927, when Supermarine was absorbed by Vickers, although Supermarine still sold aircraft under its original name. The company was, primarily, a seaplane manufacturer during this period and of the 24 aircraft Mitchell designed, most were consequently seaplanes, although he was also responsible for other designs. However, apart from his work on the Spitfire, he is best remembered for Supermarine's Schneider Trophy entries. The experience gained by Mitchell and his team in building and operating these aircraft had a significant effect on the later design of the Supermarine Spitfire fighter.

The Schneider Trophy itself was the brainchild of Jacques Schneider, a French financier, balloonist and aircraft enthusiast. The race was staged as a time-trial over a triangular course and any manufacturer or club winning the trophy three times in five years would retain it permanently.

Although Supermarine had won the

Trophy in 1922 with a biplane, the Sea Lion flying boat, Mitchell's 1925 design, the Supermarine S.4, was a much more radical aircraft, being a monoplane featuring wooden construction and a light monocoque fuselage, with unbraced cantilever wings, powered by a 680hp Napier Lion VII engine.

1. Mitchell and his production team from left to right: Mutt Summers, Agony Paine, RJ Mitchell, S. Scott and Geoffrey Quill **2.** Statue in of RJ Mitchell in Hanley **3.** Supermarine S.6B Schneider Trophy winner. Mitchell is standing behind the floats in the background **4.** Mitchell and his development and racing team in front of the 1927 Schneider entry, the S.5. Mitchell is in the centre of the picture

Unfortunately, the construction proved to be too light and, although it raised the existing world seaplane record to just under 227mph, while preparing for the American Schneider race, it crashed, ending up as a total loss.

Mitchell learned from the flaws in the S.4 and in 1927, he designed and built the Supermarine S.5. This aircraft was an all-metal monoplane aircraft with a braced, semi-monocoque fuselage and additional bracing to the internal structure of the wing, manufactured from spruce and plywood. This time Mitchell had got it right and the S.5, flown by a member of the RAF High Speed Flight, won the Venice Schneider trophy race at a speed of 281mph. The Trophy races now became bi-annual and in 1929, Mitchell did it again with a Supermarine S.6, powered by the new Rolls-Royce R engine, at a speed of 328.63mph. Unfortunately, the British Government refused to fund the next Trophy race in 1931, but public outcry and private finance resulted in the contest being reinstated, with just nine months to spare before the start of the race. Mitchell's only hope of an entry lay in modifying the S.6 to take a larger, 2,350hp version of the Rolls-Royce R, with two of the old existing S.6s also fitted

with the new power plant. Supermarine won again, retaining the Trophy permanently, despite Britain being the only competitor.

The Spitfire

In 1931 the Air Ministry, the body responsible then for managing the affairs of the RAF, issued a specification for a fighter aircraft to replace the slow and generally out-dated Gloster Gauntlet. Mitchell submitted a design, the type 244, which was rejected as too slow and lacking in manoeuvrability. By this time the Axis were all building modern aircraft, such as the Me109, featuring monocoque construction, high powered in-line liquid cooled engines, together with fully enclosed cockpits, retractable undercarriages and all-metal wings. Many in the Air Ministry however, preferred what they were familiar with, the simple cheap, slow bi-plane, so they commissioned the Gloster Gladiator as their new fighter type in 1935. However, not everybody at the Ministry was unaware of modern fighter developments, and in 1933 Supermarine authorised Mitchell to begin work on another prototype, the type 300, an all metal fighter which became the Spitfire, the prototype eventually being funded by the Air Ministry.

Mitchell began work immediately but contrary to the popular conception of the Spitfire's designer, he did not think up all the aircraft's innovative features himself. He was not hesitant about borrowing ideas from others but his genius lay in putting them all together. His Schneider Trophy experience, and knowledge gained from the Type 224, enabled his team to produce a world-class, all-metal fighter aircraft. First flown on 5 March 1936, it later reached a speed of 349mph, at which point, before the completion of official trials, the RAF demanded 310 production Spitfires. Mitchell is reported to have said, "Spitfire was just the sort of bloody silly name they would choose."

RJ Mitchel died of complications resulting from rectal cancer on 11 June 1937, aged just 42, and is buried in South Stoneham Cemetery, Hampshire.

JAMES 'JOHNNIE' JOHNSON

With 34 individual victories, all against fighters, Johnson was Britain's top scoring ace of WWII

Credited with being Britain's top scoring ace of World War II, James 'Johnnie' Johnson's flying career is a remarkable tale of exemplary professionalism and skill. Born in 1915, Johnson's early life was ordinary for a British schoolboy with a keen interest in sport, shooting and aviation. Johnson's interest in flying led him to take private flying lessons, but ultimately it was his desire to join the RAF. This wouldn't be an easy feat, particularly after a rugby injury left Johnson with an incorrectly-set collarbone. Furthermore, Johnson was initially rejected from flying service twice: firstly from the Auxiliary Air Force, a decision Johnson felt was based purely on his class status and secondly from the Royal Air Force Volunteer Reserve on the grounds that they were over prescribed and his injury made him unsuitable for pilot training. Johnson was, however, finally accepted by the RAFVR and commencing training in the August of 1939.

His flying career, like so many others, began on the de Havilland Tiger Moth, with him soloing on 29 February 1940. After passing through the Operational Training Unit, Johnson was sent for training on Spitfires, first flying the type on 19 August 1940. During training, Johnson's injury caused problems, leaving him packing his

1

shoulder with wool to ease the pain that the high-performance Spitfire created. Despite this difficulty, Johnson was posted to 616 Squadron at RAF Coltishall on 6 September 1940. It was during this time that his shoulder began to cause him immense pain, and it was decided that an operation was necessary. It wouldn't be until December 1940 that he was back flying with 616 Squadron operationally.

Johnson's first action was to come on 15 January 1941, when he and another 616 pilot, attacked a Dornier Do.17, claiming it as damaged. In March 1941 Douglas Bader came to RAF Tangmere as the new Wing Leader. Johnson was to spend most of his time flying in Bader's leading section. It was during the Circus offensives in the summer of 1941 that Johnson was to gain his first victories. On 26 June, Johnson shot down

1. Spitfire Mk XIV G-SPIT, painted in Johnson's colours for its appearance at the 2000 Flying Legends airshow **2.** A rare colour picture of Johnson with his dog in Normandy following the invasion **3.** Johnson returning to a buzz of media attention around his aircraft **4.** A Fw-190 from Johnson's gun camera. This would be his 19th victory

a Bf 109E that had the misfortune to fly in front of him and, as the intensity of the fighter sweeps increased, Johnson found himself scoring regular victories, becoming an ace on 21 September. Despite his personal successes, Johnson felt that the fighter sweeps were a waste of talented pilots. He had flown the day that Bader was lost and seen many friends downed over France for little gain. By the end of 1941, Johnson was made Flight Lieutenant and had received the DFC medal.

The later months of 1941 featured little offensive combat for Johnson, as he headed to RAF Kings Cliffe in January 1942 and it wasn't until April that he was to resume operations over France. It was in these early sweeps that Johnson first experienced the Fw-190. A superior aircraft to the Spitfire Vb's that the RAF had been flying, the Fw-190 took away the RAF's performance advantage. Johnson wouldn't score another victory till 19 August while flying cover for the disastrous Dieppe Raid. It would be a

busy morning though. During the operation he destroyed an Fw-190 and shared a Bf 109 victory. The most remarkable event however, was when Johnson was bounced by an Fw-190 and was pursued furiously from 8,000 feet down to ground level. At a severe disadvantage, he headed towards a friendly destroyer, hoping its guns would shoot down the Fw-190 and not him. His gamble worked and he returned with two more victories and an astonishing story.

The secret to Johnson's success was certainly in his excellent marksmanship. He was a natural deflection shooter and extremely well disciplined in the air. In March 1943, Johnson was promoted to Wing Leader of the Kenley wing. He changed the wing's standard formation from the line abreast to the more tactically sound Finger Four, and rejected ground attack missions for his wing wherever he could. The period that followed would be highly successful, scoring 19 victories, all against fighters.

After a six month rest, Johnson returned

to operational flying with 144 Squadron, supporting the build up for the invasion of France. Flying regularly again his score began to build and he was well liked for his strong leadership and talented shooting. After the successful Allied landings, Johnson's wing was the first to be stationed in France. From here the Spitfire's limited range was not a factor and the RAF fighters started to probe deeper into German territory. Johnson's last victory was on 27 September when he downed a Bf 109, taking his score to 34 individual victories. Remarkably, his aircraft was only hit once from enemy aircraft fire. This speaks volumes for the high level of skill he possessed as a pilot and an aerial tactician. In April 1945 he was promoted to Group Captain but, while flying regularly, he never got another opportunity to engage the Luftwaffe. He stayed in the RAF after the war, spending time with the USAF in the Korean War flying F-86's and became the AOC at RAF Cottesmore in the early 1960s.

DOUGLAS BADER

Despite losing both legs in an accident, Bader went on to serve in the RAF in WWII, becoming one of its most famous aces. He finished the war as a prisoner in Colditz Castle

Born in St. John's Wood, north-west London in 1910, Douglas Robert Steuart Bader would become one of the RAF's most famous fighter pilots of World War II. His father worked as a civil engineer in India, and it would be in this country that Douglas spent his early years. Bader, however, returned to England to attend St. Edward's School in Oxford, and, at the tender age of 11, made the decision to join the RAF. Seven years later, Bader entered the RAF College at Cranwell, where his uncle had been adjutant.

While at Cranwell, Bader was noted for being a keen sportsman, representing the college in rugby, hockey, athletics, boxing and cricket. He went on to become a prize cadet, finishing second in the contest for the sword of honour, and the college journal recorded him as having a 'no-time-to-spare' type of personality. A later, confidential report labelled him as 'plucky, capable, and headstrong'.

In August 1930, Bader was commissioned into the RAF as a Pilot Officer, being posted to No. 23 Squadron at RAF Kenley, where he flew Gloster Gamecocks and Bristol Bulldogs. He proved to be an exceptional pilot, which led to him being chosen as a display pilot for the Hendon

While at Cranwell, Bader was noted for being a very keen sportsman

1. Squadron Leader Douglas Bader with his Hawker Hurricane at Duxford, September 1940
2. Bader with pilots of No. 242 Squadron at Duxford, September 1940 3. Bader with Major Alexander 'Sasha' Hess of No. 310 (Czechoslovak) Squadron at Duxford, September 1940
4. Bader with Flight Lieutenant Eric Ball and Pilot Officer Willie McKnight at Duxford, October 1940 5. Air Chief Marshal Lord Dowding talking with Group Captain Bader and veteran fighter pilots

casualties during the Battle of France and, as a consequence, morale amongst its pilots was low. However, Bader quickly transformed the squadron and built up the confidence of the unit. His positive influence can be seen when, on 30 August, the squadron shot down a total of twelve enemy aircraft, two of which were credited to Bader. Bader was soon in command of the Duxford Wing, consisting of No. 242 and other squadrons, and would be awarded a DSO in September, followed by a DFC a month later.

It would be during the Battle of Britain that Bader became involved in controversy by siding with Air Vice-Marshall Trafford Leigh-Mallory, Commander of 12 Group, who advocated the 'big wing'. This tactic took the form of assembling three to five squadrons of fighters in order to intercept large formations of incoming German aircraft. However, Air Vice-Marshall Keith Park, the Commander of 11 Group, preferred to use single squadrons, which he felt were more flexible. This difference in approach led to much friction between Leigh-Mallory and Park.

In March 1941, Bader was promoted to Wing Commander and given command of the Tangmere wing in Sussex, which consisted of three Spitfire squadrons. He led a number of aggressive fighter sweeps across northern France and, despite the fact his squadrons were re-equipped with MK VB Spitfires – armed with two 20mm cannons and four .303 machineguns – Bader insisted his own aircraft remained armed with eight machineguns, which he believed was more effective for the tactics he employed.

Bader would receive a bar to both his DSO and DFC, as well as the French Croix de Guerre and Légion d'Honneur. However, his luck ran out on 9 August 1941 when he was shot down near St. Omer in the Pas-de-Calais. He managed to bail out and successfully deployed his parachute, but he lost his right leg in the process. Knocked unconscious upon landing, he awoke to find himself taken prisoner of war by two German soldiers.

His missing leg was recovered from the wreckage of his Spitfire and repaired (the RAF later parachuted him a replacement), after which he promptly attempted to escape. Recaptured, he was sent to Oflag VIB, then Stalag Luft III and Stalag Luft VIIIB. During this time, he again attempted to escape and ended up being imprisoned in Colditz Castle, where he remained until he was liberated in April 1945.

Returning to Britain he was promoted to Group Captain but eventually left the RAF in March 1946, after which he re-joined Shell. In 1956 he was made a CBE and knighted in 1976. He died in 1982, aged 72.

Air Show. However, in December 1931 Bader, flying a Bulldog at Woodley Aerodrome, crashed while performing low-level aerobatics. Although he survived the accident, he had to have both legs amputated.

Despite this, Bader was determined to walk again, using artificial limbs without recourse to a walking stick, something he successfully achieved. He further demonstrated that he could meet the demanding requirements the RAF placed on its pilots, but the medical board refused to let him fly. As a result, he was discharged from the RAF in 1933, after which he took up a position with the Asiatic Petroleum Company (Shell).

In the summer of 1939, Bader realised that war was on the horizon and sought to re-join the RAF as a pilot. Demonstrating he still had a talent for flying, he was sent on a refresher course in November and posted to No. 19 Squadron at Duxford the

In the summer of 1939, Bader realised that war was on the horizon

following February with the rank of Flying Officer. Six weeks later he was posted to command A Flight of No. 222 Squadron, and, as a Flight Lieutenant, experienced action while flying a Spitfire near Dunkirk during the evacuation of the BEF in 1940. On 24 June, he was made Acting Squadron Leader of No. 242 (Canadian) Squadron based at Coltishall in Norfolk.

No. 242 Squadron had suffered heavy

GUY GIBSON

The man who led the most audacious bombing mission of World War II was initially rejected by the RAF

G uy Penrose Gibson was born in Simla, India in 1918. His father worked for the Indian forest service, and would be a cold and remote figure in Gibson's early life, while his mother was a self-absorbed alcoholic. Unsurprisingly, his parents' marriage was an unhappy one and, in 1924, his mother returned to England taking her children with her. As a result of his difficult childhood, Gibson would become emotionally insecure and in later life felt compelled to prove himself. Nevertheless, he would go on to lead what was, perhaps, the most daring bomber raid of the entire Second World War and be awarded the Victoria Cross for it.

Between 1926 and 1932, Gibson attended St. George's Preparatory School in Folkestone, Kent. He was not noted for being particularly academic, but was viewed as being both hard working and determined. Gibson sought a career in the RAF but was rejected for being too short – he was 5ft 6in – but he tried again. In 1936 he was finally accepted into the force and began training as a pilot.

Graduating from 6 Flying Training School in August 1937, where he was rated 'average', he was posted to No. 83 Squadron at RAF Turnhouse in Scotland. In March the following year, his squadron received Hawker Hind bombers and moved to RAF Scampton in Lincolnshire. By December, the squadron had been re-equipped with Handley Page Hampden bombers.

Gibson would be serving with No. 83 Squadron upon the outbreak of World War II, completing 37 operational flights by the time he was posted to 14 Operational Training Unit in Cottesmore in September

> **Gibson sought a career in the RAF but was rejected for being too short**

1940. During this time, he was also awarded the DFC. Gibson's new posting lasted a mere two weeks due to the chronic shortage of night-fighter pilots. He was posted to No. 29 Squadron at RAF Digby, which was equipped with Bristol Blenheims, although the unit then slowly received the newer Bristol Beaufighters.

On 14 March 1941, Gibson shot down an enemy bomber, downing a further three following the squadron's move to RAF West Malling in Kent in April. By June, Gibson had been promoted to Squadron Leader and, in September, awarded a bar to his DFC. With his latest tour expired, he was posted as Chief Flying Instructor to 51 Operational Training Unit at Cranfield.

Disliking instructing, Gibson was given command of No. 106 Squadron at RAF Coningsby in April 1942 with the rank of Wing Commander. At this time the squadron was equipped with the underpowered Avro Manchester, but it was subsequently re-equipped with the highly successful Avro Lancaster. Within months, Gibson made the squadron the best

1. Wing Commander Guy Gibson was awarded the Victoria Cross for leading the Dam Busters raid 2. Gibson taking a rare moment to relax between flying operations in 1943 3. Gibson's Avro Lancaster fitted with 'Upkeep', known as the bouncing bomb 4. Gibson and his crew board their Avro Lancaster for the raid on the Ruhr Dams 5. Wing Commander Guy Gibson in his flying gear sometime in 1943 6. Gibson (second from left) with King George VI (centre) inspecting a model of the Möhne

performing unit of 5 Group, an achievement which led to the award of a DSO. When he completed the tour, he had made 72 sorties and received a bar to his DSO.

Normally a period of rest would follow such service, but Gibson was instead asked to form a new squadron for a special mission. The squadron would be numbered 617, and it would conduct one of the most famous bombing raids of the entire war which became known as the Dam Busters.

The purpose of the raid was to cause disruption to German industry in the Ruhr. In order to do this a number of key dams were to be destroyed. Time, however, was of the essence as the dams had to be attacked when the moon was brightest and the dams were full. This gave Gibson only two months in which to form and train an entirely new

squadron in the tactics necessary.

To destroy the dams a new weapon was required. This was designed by engineer Barnes Wallis, who came up with the idea of a bouncing bomb that could skip across water to sink moored battleships. It was quickly realised that the bomb could also be used against the dams. Codenamed 'Upkeep', tests revealed that the drum-shaped bomb would need to be released from a height of 60ft while at a ground speed of 232mph. The bomb would then spin backwards across the surface of the water to the dam wall, where its residual spin would push the bomb down the wall for it to explode at its base.

At 9:28pm on 16 May 1943, Gibson led 19 Lancasters with 133 crew in three waves towards the dams. Gibson, in the first wave, attacked the Möhne dam, but it would take

five attempts by five bombers to breach it. An attack was then made on the Eder dam, which was similarly breached, but the attacks on the Scorpe dam failed. Some 53 men of Gibson's force were killed, while 1,300 people died on the ground from the subsequent flooding below the dams.

In truth, the success of the mission rested in the morale boosting effect it had on the British people, since the damage done to German industry was modest. Nevertheless, Gibson was seen as a national hero and awarded the Victoria Cross.

On the night of 19 September 1944, while returning from a raid just a few miles inside German territory, Gibson's De Havilland Mosquito crashed near Steenbergen in the Netherlands and exploded, killing him. He was aged just 26.

ARTHUR HARRIS

A tough talking commander who remains one of the most controversial figures in RAF history

Born in Cheltenham in 1892, Sir Arthur 'Bomber' Harris is, perhaps, one of the most controversial figures in RAF history for the bombing tactics he employed against Germany. Harris' father was an engineer and architect in India, while his mother was the daughter of a surgeon in the Madras cavalry. Despite his family living and working in India, Harris was sent to England for his education, attending Allhallows School in Honiton, Devon. As a result of this separation from his parents, he would quickly grow to become exceptionally self-reliant.

At the age of 17, Harris, against the wishes of his father, travelled to Rhodesia in the hope of becoming a goldminer, although he also worked as a coach driver and farmer. When World War I broke out, Harris decided to join the newly formed 1st Rhodesian Regiment, in which he served as a bugler. The regiment, however, was short-lived, being disbanded the following year, and so Harris travelled back to England to enlist in the British Army.

Unable to enter the cavalry or artillery, Harris joined the Royal Flying Corps, being commissioned as a Second Lieutenant in November 1915. He had obtained a civilian pilot's licence from the Royal Aero Club following half an hour's tuition at Brooklands. During the war, he would serve as a night-fighter pilot in defence against Zeppelins, later being given command of No. 38 Squadron. However, he would eventually go to France with No. 70 Squadron, but returned following a crash in which he was injured. Despite this, he returned to France in May 1917 with No. 45 Squadron. Harris was noted for being strict, but also an effective pilot who achieved five aerial victories. He was awarded an AFC in 1918.

Between the World Wars, Harris continued to serve in the newly formed Royal Air Force, commanding a number of squadrons abroad and a flying school at home. He was made an OBE in 1927, and the following year attended the Army Staff College where he was taught by Bernard Montgomery. Later, he joined the Air Ministry, serving as Deputy Director of operations and intelligence, then Deputy Director of plans. During this time, Harris became an advocate for the proposal of four-engined heavy bombers, arguing that air power was key to victory and would help avoid the need for pointless trench warfare.

In 1937, he left the Air Ministry to take command of No. 4 (Bomber) Group and was promoted to Commodore. The following year, however, he went to the

Harris became an advocate for the proposal of four-engined heavy bombers

USA to examine aircraft and recommend purchases, after which he became Air Officer commanding Palestine and Transjordan. In 1938, he would be promoted again, this time to Air Vice-Marshal.

Following the outbreak of World War II, Harris was given command of No. 5 (Bomber) Group, its headquarters being at Grantham, Lincolnshire. Due to losses during daylight operations, the Handley Page Hampden bombers of the group switched to night time raids, a tactic Harris had long advocated. During his time with the group, Harris gained a reputation of being particularly tough, but he was also noted for his efficient organisational skills.

In 1940 Harris was made a CB and asked

1. Harris, Graham and Saundby studying a wall map at High Wycombe **2.** Harris (seated) with Air Vice-Marshal Ronald Graham (left) and Air Vice-Marshal Robert Saundby (middle) **3.** Harris watches as Guy Gibson's crew is debriefed following the raid on the Ruhr Dams **4.** Harris studies aerial reconnaissance photos at his High Wycombe Headquarters **5.** Harris at his desk at Bomber Command Headquarters at High Wycombe

by Chares Portal, the Commander-in-Chief of Bomber Command, to act as his deputy. However, bureaucratic work at the Air Ministry did not sit well with Harris, and so, in May 1941, he was sent to the USA in order to speed up the supply of aircraft and other supplies. Again, Harris was successful in his latest mission, but he would be recalled to England in February 1942 to take up the position of Commander-in-Chief of Bomber Command, being formally appointed on the 23rd of the month.

Until this point, Bomber Command had not been the effective fighting force that it became later in the war. All this changed under Harris, who sought to introduce new, bigger four-engined bombers such as the Avro Lancaster, new tactical procedures and worked to raise morale amongst the bomber crews. Although he spoke his mind, usually bluntly, and refused to suffer fools, he turned Bomber Command into a highly effective striking force by 1943.

Despite this, Harris has been, and continues to be, highly criticised for his policy of bombing German cities and killing many thousands of German civilians. This policy was aimed at destroying German morale following the apparent inability of Bomber Command to accurately hit and destroy German military or economic targets. However, it should be noted that this policy was initiated in 1941, before Harris took command, although he did ruthlessly pursue it once in post.

Harris himself did not believe destroying German morale alone would win the war. British bombers needed to target German industry, thus forcing the country to its knees. This, however, he argued could not be achieved by bombing just specific targets. Rather, a wider, more general, bombing campaign of attrition against Germany was required. Thus, he opposed operations such as the Dam Busters raid but encouraged the so-called 1,000 bomber raids.

He retired from the RAF in 1946, and wrote the Bomber Offensive, in which he robustly defended his wartime tactics. Harris died in 1984 and is buried at Burntwood Cemetery, Goring.

PAULINE GOWER

A true pioneer of early flight who established the female section of the Air Transport Auxiliary, responsible for ferrying aircraft to frontline squadrons

Pauline Mary de Peauly Gower was born in 1910 at Tunbridge Wells, Kent. Her father, Sir Robert Gower, was a solicitor and Conservative MP, while her mother, Dorothy, was the daughter of Herbert Wills JP. Her privileged, well-connected background allowed Gower to enjoy a comfortable life near her native Tunbridge Wells, where her family resided in a large house. Although a non-Catholic, Gower was educated at the local Beechwood Sacred Heart Convent, where she demonstrated that she was an able student with a personality that made her popular amongst fellow pupils and staff.

Following her education, Gower travelled to London where he explored subjects such as music, photography, horse riding and even politics, but the thought of becoming a pilot greatly appealed to her. Gower's father disapproved of her flying and refused to fund her lessons, so she raised the necessary money by offering violin lessons. Incredibly, she made her first solo flight after only seven hours flying time. Gower received her flying certificate from the Phillips and Powis School of Aviation following a mere 15 hours and 15 minutes in the air.

Gower would go on to gain her commercial pilots licence, and would become friends with Dorothy Spicer. The two later went into business, establishing an air joyriding company, hiring a Gipsy Moth and later purchasing a two-seater Simmonds Spartan; Gower would be the pilot while Spicer acted as engineer. Ironically, this latter aircraft was bought using funds supplied by Gower's father, who eventually became

Gower (second from left) with female Polish pilots of the ATA

supportive of her flying career. In 1932, with Gower just 22, the pair joined the Crimson Fleet, an air circus, before setting up Air Trips Ltd, another joyriding and air-taxi service that was based at Hunstanton, Norfolk. It was the first aviation company to be entirely owned by women.

Tragedy, however, struck when Gower learned that her mother had unexpectedly died, and so she gave up touring in order to

support her grief-stricken father. It would also not be long before Gower and Spicer took the decision to dissolve their business, finding their work no longer satisfying. They did, however, jointly write a book entitled Women with Wings, which was published in 1938. However, Pauline's flying career was not over yet, and she was soon to embark upon, perhaps, the most important work of her life.

1. A Simmonds Spartan two-seat biplane, similar to that flown by Gower and Spicer **2.** Gower with fellow female pilots of the ATA and an Avro AnsonPauline **3.** Gower in a Tiger Moth, one of many aircraft types she flew during her career **4.** Period newspaper cutting of Gower 'Commander of the Air Transport Auxiliary (Women's Section)'

They Deliver the 'Planes

Miss Pauline Gower (left), Commander of the Air Transport Auxiliary (Women's Section), with Miss Jacqueline Cochrane, Flight Captain of the American Women Pilots' Section. The Air Transport Auxiliary is the service responsible for ferrying 'planes from the factories to the R.A.F.

With the outbreak of World War II, Gower became a member of the Air Transport Auxiliary (ATA), a civilian service that undertook the task of ferrying military aircraft from their factories to frontline squadrons, thus freeing up RAF pilots. Despite opposition from those who believed women were unsuited to flying, a persuasive Gower, using her connections, was, on 14 December 1939, given permission to appoint eight women pilots to the ATA. These carefully hand-picked aviators, all of who had much flying experience, were revealed to the world during a press launch in January the following year.

By May, the ATA was made responsible for ferrying most military aircraft, and as a consequence the service had begun to experience rapid expansion. In addition to the growing number of pilots, additional drivers, engineers, ground support and medical personnel also joined. Those who entered the service came from all over the world, including recruits from Canada, Australia and the United States, amongst numerous other countries. Even men and women from occupied nations such as the Netherlands, Poland and Denmark donned the ATA uniform.

During the Battle of France and the subsequent Battle of Britain, losses sustained by the RAF placed further demands on the ATA. At this time, female pilots of the service were only allowed to fly training aircraft, but in 1941, at the height of the Blitz, they were finally given permission to ferry fighter aircraft to frontline squadrons. Later in the war, some of the women, thanks to Gower's constant pressure on the authorities, were trained to fly heavier aircraft, including bombers.

As the war progressed, many more women pilots joined, with in excess of 160 serving in the ATA during the war. As senior commander and director of women personnel, Gower personally selected and tested all female pilots for entry into the ATA. Some 15 women of the ATA lost their lives during the conflict, including flight pioneer, Amy Johnson. One important landmark was that in 1943 the Government awarded the women of the ATA the same pay as the men for doing the same job.

Gower received an MBE for her work in 1942, and the following year she was made a director of British Overseas Airways, becoming the first women to hold such a senior position in a national airline. In 1945, she became engaged to Wing Commander William Fahie, marrying later that year.

Tragically, on 2 March 1947, Pauline Gower suddenly died of a heart attack at her home in Chelsea, after having just given birth to twin boys. She was buried a few days later in her native Tunbridge Wells.

CAPTAIN ERIC MELROSE 'WINKLE' BROWN

A legend of British aviation who had a Royal Navy commission but contributed to all the flying services, including the RAF. His record as a test pilot was nothing short of incredible

Captain Brown at his desk, during his time serving at RNAS Lossiemouth in 1967

Eric Brown was an iconic figure in British aviation and held multiple flying records including the most carrier landings in history and being the only British pilot to fly the Luftwaffe ME163 Komet rocket plane. Officially, he was a Fleet Air Arm pilot and held a Royal Navy commission for his whole career but his extensive contribution to all aspects of British aviation, including flying combat missions for the Canadians and the RAF, and his astonishing record as a test pilot, transcended any specific service.

Brown was initiated into the aviation world, surprisingly, in Germany where he was introduced to powered flight by World War I fighter ace Ernst Udet. He was also a personal friend of Hannah Reitsch who he met at a 1938 automobile exhibition where she flew an early FW61 helicopter inside the Deutschlandhalle. Brown was a fluent German speaker and was actually in Germany on an educational exchange visit when war was declared. He was duly detained for several days by the SS which, after some deliberation, escorted him in his MG car to the Swiss border informing him

Lt Cdr Brown in the cockpit of an aircraft after a successful carrier landing

he was free to go and he could keep his car as they were unable to get any spares for it.

On his return to wartime Britain, Brown joined the Royal Navy Volunteer Reserve as a Fleet Air Arm pilot joining 802 Squadron based the convoy escort carrier HMS *Audacity*. During this deployment Brown perfected a head on attack method against the Focke-Wulf Kurier (Condor) bombers,

which were harassing convoys, as this was the least defended part of the heavily armed machines. However the *Audacity* didn't survive the war and was torpedoed by U751 in 1941 whilst Brown was stationed aboard. He subsequently spent 24 hours in the water awaiting rescue and, when recovered, was suffering from advanced hypothermia. For his actions on HMS *Audacity*, Eric Brown was subsequently awarded the Distinguished Service Cross.

Between this time and Brown joining the RAE in 1943 he was seconded to the Royal Canadian Air Force flying bomber escort missions over Germany where his role was to train pilots to deck-land on

A captured Fiat CR-42, test flown by Brown who was impressed by its manoeuvrability but noted that it was woefully underarmed

1. The high-speed DH 108 VW120 that Eric Brown flew. This aircraft later crashed, killing Brown's successor at the RAE, Sqn. Ldr. Stuart Muller-Rowland
2. A captured He 177 A-5 in British markings flown by Eric Brown at RAE Farnborough in September 1944
3. 3 December 1945, Eric Brown became the first pilot to land on and take off from an aircraft carrier in a jet-engined aircraft when he flew a de Havilland Sea Vampire to HMS Ocean

carriers (simulated on airfields). He also joined the Canadians in multiple combat bomber escort missions during this period. Subsequently on joining the RAE he was immediately posted to southern Italy with the task of evaluating captured Italian and German aircraft.

Brown's ability to master these foreign machines with little documentation or instruction was soon noted by his commander and resulted in a posting to the RAE in Farnborough where he duly established the record for the most carrier landings, carried out by a pilot, and tested multiple aircraft types in this role, including the Mosquito.

During this time at RAE, Brown also flew missions for RAF Fighter Command and his own house was destroyed in 1944 by a V1 doodlebug concussing his wife and seriously injuring their cleaning lady.

Arguably, Eric Brown's most famous actions during the war were evaluation flights for the RAE of captured German aircraft including the ME262 Jet Fighter, Arado Blitz Jet Bomber and the Komet ME163 rocket fighter as well as the time he spent in Germany retrieving and securing these aircraft for the Allies. What is less known is that due to his ability to speak fluent German he was also with the first Allied troops to enter Bergen Belsen concentration camp, thanks to a request from Brigadier Glyn Hughes to assist with the interrogation of captured SS guards. During this time he carried out the interrogations of Josef Kramer and Irma Grese who he described as the most

Eric in his later years, recounting his various adventures, including landing on an aircraft carrier for the first time

disgusting human beings he'd ever met. On a similar note Brown also interviewed Hermann Goering when he was awaiting trial at Nuremburg and was requested to do so from the point of view of a pilot. When Goering realised he was addressing a fellow flier, Brown recounted the conversation became very amiable and the two men were able to relate their shared flying experiences. Goering offered Brown his hand at the end of the meeting which Brown refused, instead replying with, "Hals und Beinbruch!" This was the German World War I fighter pilot greeting, meaning, "Broken legs and broken neck!" It was an expression he'd first heard from Udet in better times, before the war.

Brown's nickname of 'Winkle', came from

his short stature and ability to fit into small spaces. It was the reason for his survival in numerous aircraft incidents where a taller man would have perished. The most famous example of this was his flight in the De Havilland DH108 in 1946 where he was attempting to break the sound barrier. This aircraft had killed its previous pilot, the famous Geoffrey De Havilland Jr and almost accounted for Brown as well as due to a high G-pitch oscillation at Mach 0.985 which snapped the neck of the significantly-taller man. Brown was able to recover the aircraft and report back on the problem because of his flying skill and to a large degree, his shorter neck.

The achievements of Captain Eric Brown are too vast to list in this short piece with his record for flying the most types of aircraft – some 487 – is unlikely to ever be equalled again. He was truly a giant of British aviation whose contributions advanced our knowledge of flight and aircraft capabilities for all the British services.

FRANK WHITTLE

Dogged designer, skilled pilot and the man who revolutionised flight by giving Britain her first jet aircraft

1. Air Commodore, Sir Frank Whittle, sat at his desk, working **2.** The test bed for Whittle's revolutionary new engine was the Gloster E.28/39 **3.** Britain's first jet-powered fighter plane, the Gloster Meteor **4.** Frank Whittle's first successful jet engine

During WWII there was a secret battle fought by scientists and designers from Britain and Nazi Germany. The winner would be the first to successfully field a jet aircraft. At the centre of Britain's effort was a small, but driven, man from Coventry; Frank Whittle.

Born in June 1907, Whittle dreamed of becoming a fighter pilot from a young age. Deeply interested in engineering and science at 16 he passed the RAF's entrance exam to become an aircraft apprentice. Unfortunately, his slender stature meant he failed his medical but Whittle was determined and put himself through a strict exercise regime and diet to pass. He finally entered the RAF's technical school and his keen intellect and interest in aviation science saw him recommended for officer training.

In 1928, aged just 21, Whittle graduated from RAF College Cranwell, second in his class, writing a detailed thesis on possible future developments in aircraft design. He also finally achieved his dream of learning to fly, becoming an accomplished pilot. He was later posted to the Central Flying School as an instructor and almost joined the RAF display flying team in 1930.

During this time Whittle began to formulate the idea of using a jet turbine instead of a conventional combustion engine. In 1930, he patented his idea but the RAF and Air Ministry showed little interest in his design believing it impractical. In 1932, Whittle enrolled on the RAF's Officer's Engineering

Course and having excelled he was given leave to take a two-year engineering course at Cambridge, from which he graduated with a First.

With the RAF still not interested in his ideas Whittle, and some colleagues, founded Power Jets Ltd in 1936. The company went on to develop the basis of the jet engine idea. At the same time, German engineers were also working on the concept of a jet engine and financial difficulties slowed Power Jets' work, despite Whittle and his team working long hours.

Finally, just months before the outbreak of war the Air Ministry took interest in Whittle's engine. They began to fund development and contracted Gloster to build a test-bed aircraft for the new engine – the Gloster E.28/39.

Whittle pushed himself to the edge trying to ready his engine and, in late 1940, he suffered a nervous breakdown, due in part to a reliance on amphetamines to keep him going during the long hours spent in the lab. After a month's rest, he was able to return to work and by early 1941 the Gloster E.28/39 began undergoing its first engine tests. The E.28/39 flew for the first time on 15 May, 1941, powered by Whittle's revolutionary new jet engine.

Despite Whittle's efforts the Luftwaffe beat him getting the Me262 into action in April 1944. The Gloster Meteor, Britian's first operational jet fighter, was introduced several months later in June. Both jets saw

combat during the war but never against one another. While the Me262 enjoyed some success, its engines were prone to overheating. For his efforts, Whittle was promoted to Air Commodore after the war. He was awarded a knighthood, the order of the Bath, the American Legion of Merit and the prestigious Rumford Medal. Whittle retired from the RAF in 1948. Later, he worked for a number of private companies including BOAC, Bristol Aero Engines and then as a professor at the US Naval Academy. He died in 1996, aged 89.

Find the hidden story in your family's past with
the essential resource for all family historians

9:41 AM

iPad 📶

BRINGING YOU EXPERT ADVICE FOR OVER 30 YEARS

www.family-tree.co.uk

Family Tree

MARCH 2017

TRACE BACK TO THE 1500s
15 KEY RECORDS TO TAKE YOUR RESEARCH BACK TO TUDOR TIMES

HAPPY 100TH DAME VERA
Celebrating a centenary of the Forces' Sweetheart

New to family history?
5 ESSENTIAL WEBSITES TO TRY TODAY!

FREE RECORDS EXPLAINED
How to find your IRISH RELATIONS

INVESTIGATING
culture & lives in post-World War 2 Britain

Plus
• Track down your railway ancestors
• Wartime style & 1940s fashion

9 770267 113225

Visit www.familytreedigital.com today!

SOPWITH CAMEL

The Sopwith Camel was a multi-purpose aircraft that served with the RFC and then the RAF. Highly manoeuvrable, if dangerous in the hands of a novice, its pilots shot down over 1,000 enemy aircraft

Built by the Sopwith Aviation Company, the Camel was a successor to the earlier Pup and had the same conventional design of wooden box fuselage, aluminium engine cowling, and fabric-covered fuselage, wings and tail. It also had a humped metal fairing over the gun breeches, which led to pilots naming it the Camel, although this was never an official designation. The close proximity of the engine, pilot, guns and fuel tank made it extremely manoeuvrable, and although its flying characteristics could make it dangerous in the hands of a novice pilot, with a simple stall rapidly developing into a dangerous spin, many experienced pilots were complimentary about the type. During its service with the RFC and RAF, its pilots shot down 1,294 enemy aircraft of all types, while the Camel served as fighter, night fighter, carrier and ground-attack aircraft.

RAF planes through the years

1918

Sopwith 1½ Strutter
A single or two seat multi-role biplane that was introduced in 1916 but obsolete as a fighter by 1917. For the RAF in 1918 was used as a trainer.

1918

Fairy III
Reconnaissance aircraft, in both land and seaplance variants. The IIIF version was a two-seater used by the RAF, especially in the inter-war years.

Avro 504
Fighter, bomber and trainer from WWI.

Royal Aircraft Factory B.E.2
Recon, light bomber and night fighter.

Bristol F.2 Fighter
Agile and robust WWI fighter and recon.

Sopwith Camel F.1

TOP SPEED: 113mph
ARMAMENT: Two .303in Vickers machine guns. Some types also fitted with a Lewis gun mounted in front of the pilot on the top wing
BOMB LOAD: Four Cooper bombs
ENGINE: Clerget 9B 9-cylinder rotary engine, 130hp
NUMBER BUILT: Approximately 5,490 produced
DESIGNER: Herbert Smith

1918

Martinsyde F.4 Buzzard
Developed privately, the F.4 was the fastest fighter of WWI at 142mph. Only a few were built by the end of the war and it was then dropped by the RAF

1918

Sopwith Camel
Successor to the Pup, it was introduced in 1917 and flown by the new RAF in 1918. It feature twin-synchronised guns but was notoriously difficult to fly fo novices

Fairey Campania
Seaplane introduced by the RNAS

Sopwith T.1 Cuckoo
Biplane torpedo bomber

Sopwith 5F.1 Dolphin

HAWKER HURRICANE

The multi-role fighter was the workhorse of the RAF, serving in a variety of theatres

The prototype Hurricane first flew on 6 November 1935, and the type became the RAF's first modern monoplane fighter with eight guns and a retractable undercarriage. The first RAF unit to operate Hurricanes was 111 Squadron at Northolt which received its first aircraft in December 1937. The Hurricane achieved much in its service: it shot down more enemy aircraft during the Battle of Britain than any other defence asset; it destroyed more enemy aircraft than any other Allied fighter during World War II; and it served in more theatres of war than any other Allied fighter – from the Battle of France to Malta, the Western Desert, Russia and South-East Asia.

The Hurricane was used to take on the bombers of the Luftwaffe in the Battle of Britain while the Spitfire handled the fighters

LF363

YBO

1918

Airco DH.4
Two seater bomber, entered service in 1917 with the RFC, then adopted by the RAF. Most were build in the US for the American forces in France.

1918

Airco DH.6
Military training biplane first flew in 1916 with the RFC. Cheap to build and maintain as well as safe for novices to learn to fly on. Over 1,000 in use with the RAF by 1918.

Airco DH.9
Biplane bomber based on the DH.4.

Airco DH.10 Amiens
WWI twin-engined medium bomber.

Royal Aircraft Factory F.E.2d
Three different airplane designs from WWI.

VITAL STATS
HURRICANE MK.I

TOP SPEED: 324mph
ARMAMENT: Eight wing-mounted Browning 0.303in machine-guns
ENGINE: One Rolls-Royce Merlin II or III 12-cylinder, liquid cooled
supercharged inline
NUMBER BUILT: 14,500+ **DESIGNER:** Sydney Camm
SERVICE LIFE: December 1937 to February 1947

1918

Felixstowe F.2
Flying boat introduced in 1917 with the
RNAS then adopted by the RAF in 1918.
Excellent performance, used as a patrol
aircraft over the North Sea.

1918

Armstrong Whitworth F.K.8
Two seater recon/bomber biplane with
dual controls. More popular than the contemporary R.E.8. Post-war use by QANTAS
and Paraguay government.

Felixstowe F.3
Heavier, slower version with more range.

Felixstowe F.5
RAF's standard flying boat until 1925.

Blackburn Kangaroo
Late-war anti-submarine biplane.

SUPERMARINE SPITFIRE

Spitfire XIX PM631 of the Battle of
Britain Memorial Flight being flown by
Sqn Ldr Ian Smith MBE (Jarrod Cotter)

1918

Bristol M.1 Monoplane Scout
Fast monoplane, served mainly in Middle
East and Balklans in 1918. 12 were sent to
Chile in 1918 as part payment for a two
battleships being built for the navy.

1918

Handley Page Type O
Early biplane heavy bomber. Used for
strategic bombing of industrial targets in
Germany as well as tactical night attacks.
Retired in 1922.

Norman Thompson N.T.2B
Single engine flying boat trainer.

Royal Aircraft Factory R.E.8
Two-seater recon/bomber from WWI.

Sopwith Salamander
Ground attack biplane with armour.

Designed by RJ Mitchell and first flown in March 1936, the Supermarine Spitfire is one of the most iconic aircraft in the world. It fought with the RAF from the beginning of World War II until the end, having its performance and capability developed throughout

VITAL STATS

SPITFIRE MK.IA
TOP SPEED: 364mph **SERVICE CEILING:** 32,000ft
ARMAMENT: Eight wing-mounted 0.303in machine guns
ENGINE: Rolls-Royce Merlin III
NUMBER BUILT: 20,351 (total number, all Marks)
DESIGNER: RJ Mitchell **SERVICE LIFE:** August 1938 to April 1954 (all Marks)

1918

Royal Aircraft Factory S.E.5
Fast and nimble, described as the 'Spitfire of World War One'. Introduced in March 1917, served with RAF until end of war and was adopted for civilian use.

1918

Sopwith Snipe
Late-war single seat, biplane fighter with excellent climb and manoeuvrability. It was more than a match for German planes. Served with RAF until 1926.

Spad S.XIII
Mass-produced French fighter.

Vickers Vimy
Scarce, late-war heavy bomber.

Nieuport 17 C.1
French fighter used later as a trainer.

THE SPITFIRE IN FOCUS

P re-eminent among British fighters, the prototype Spitfire K5054 first flew from Eastleigh on 5 March 1936. Its successful design was born from RJ Mitchell's winning Schneider Trophy monoplane racer designs, and subsequent developments of the fighter established and maintained the air superiority that was vital to the defence of the United Kingdom from 1939. It was the Spitfire that took on the fighters of the Luftwaffe.

The first Spitfires were first delivered to No.19 Squadron at RAF Duxford in August 1938. These early Mk.Is featured a broad, two-bladed fixed-pitch propeller which was soon replaced by a three-bladed, variable-pitch propeller for improved performance. A higher powered variant of the Rolls-Royce Merlin engine also soon followed and it was with Mk.Is and Mk.IIs in this guise which RAF

Fighter Command Spitfires fought in the Battle of Britain in 1940. By the beginning of the Battle of Britain there were 19 operational squadrons equipped with Spitfires, and while the type did not win the aerial conflict alone, the Spitfire certainly made its mark as the RAF's most advanced fighter of its time.

By 1941 RAF Fighter Command had gone over to the offensive, carrying out fighter sweeps over occupied France. This was done with the next major variant of the Spitfire, the Mk.V. The Mk.Vb was a much improved variant of the Spitfire used by home-based squadrons, fitted with a powerful Merlin 45 engine and armed with two cannons and four machine-guns. The Mk.V soon dominated fighter squadrons in Northern Europe and during 1941/42 this variant was used to fly countless 'Rhubarb', 'Circus' and 'Rodeo' missions

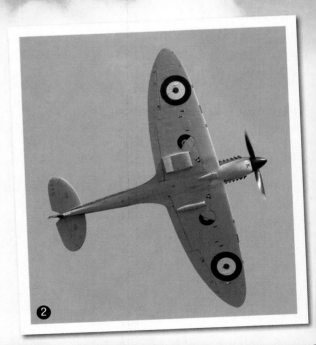

1919

Parnall Panther
Carrier-based spotter and recon aircraft that could be folded up and stored. Served on HMS **Argus** and **Hermes** and was only

1919

Sopwith Dragon
Single seat fighter, based on the Sopwith Snipe. Problems with the engine caused the RAF order to be cancelled. Second

Nieuport Nighthawk
Biplane fighter with unreliable engines.

Westland Walrus
Spotter/recon plane delivered in 1921.

Avros Bison
Carrier-based spotter/recon biplane

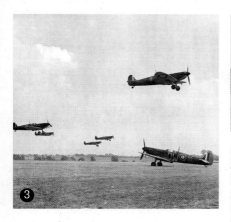

over enemy occupied territory.

The Spitfire V was more than a match for the Messerschmitt Bf 109E, although the introduction of the Bf 109F saw parity resumed in the air. However, at the end of 1941 the Focke-Wulf Fw 190A came on stream and proved more capable than the Spitfire V. In reply the Spitfire IX was developed, initially as an interim but was nothing of the sort as things worked out.

The Mk.IX featured a 1,660hp Merlin 61 engine with a two speed, two-stage supercharger driving a four-bladed propeller. The Spitfire XVI was very similar to the Mk.IX, except that it was fitted with an American Packard-built Merlin 266. The Mk.XVI was also the first variant of the Spitfire to be fitted with the 'teardrop' style canopy and a low back fuselage for improved rearward vision.

Meanwhile work was under way to fit the Spitfire with the very powerful Rolls-Royce Griffon engine. Fitting this meant an extended front end of around 2ft, and it was first developed as the Mk.XII and XIV fighter variants. However, it was an unarmed variant, the Photographic Reconnaissance PR.XIX, which became, perhaps, the most well known of all the Griffon-powered examples.

The PR.XIX became a very efficient aircraft. Having no weighty armament, and a pressurised canopy, its pilots could fly fast, alone and at high altitude to get the vital photographs needed to plan attacks, record the results of those attacks and take note of where enemy concentrations of troops, fuel and supplies were.

The last fighter versions of the Spitfire, none of which saw squadron service during World War II, were the Griffon-powered MKs.XVIII, F.21, F.22 and F.24. The last F.24, VN496, left the South Marston factory in February 1948 bringing to a close Spitfire production which had lasted just over ten years. These powerful fighters were almost at the zenith of piston-engine performance and were a match for the early jets of the RAF.

The last ever operational sortie by an RAF Spitfire was made by a PR.XIX of 81 Squadron based a Seletar in Singapore during the Malayan Campaign. The aircraft was PS888 and the sortie took place on 1 April 1954, when it flew a photographic reconnaissance mission over an area of jungle in Johore thought to contain hideouts of Communist guerrillas. Such was the occasion that the Spitfire's ground crew painted the inscription 'The Last!' on the port side engine cowling.

The Spitfire therefore had a 16 operational year career with the RAF, which represents extraordinary longevity considering the rapid developments that were made in military aviation during the war and with the advent of the jet age. In his book Fight for the Sky, Sir Douglas Bader sums up what the Spitfire achieved: 'I have

1. Spitfire IX MK356 of the Battle of Britain Memorial Flight being flown by Flt Lt Antony Parkinson MBE (Jarrod Cotter) **2.** The Spitfire has iconic elliptical wings, as clearly shown in this view of Mk.II P7350 (Jarrod Cotter) **3.** Squadron scramble as Spitfire Is take off from an airfield in southern England during the Battle of Britain (British Official) **4.** The Spitfire's very clean profile is seen to good effect here in this view of prototype K5054 (Air Ministry) **5.** Spitfire Is of No. 610 (County of Chester) Squadron patrol from RAF Hornchurch in the summer of 1940 (British Official) **6.** Spitfire I K9795 of No. 19 Squadron, the first RAF unit to receive the type (British Official) **7.** Spitfire F.22 PK312 with a teardrop canopy and lengthened front end to accommodate the Griffon engine (British Official) **8.** A war-torn looking Spitfire Vb R6923 of No. 92 Squadron based at Biggin Hill seen in 1941 (British Official)

often wondered who the genius was, who christened it Spitfire. It was a name that resounded around the free world in those dark days of Hitler's tyranny, and perfectly symbolised the mood of Britain's defence... The word "Spitfire" became synonymous with eventual freedom to the citizens of occupied countries across the English Channel and North Sea. It was a symbol that good would triumph over evil.'

1921

Vickers Vernon
A large biplane for carrying troops - the first such dedicated troop transport for the RAF. Entered service in 1921. Airlifted 500 troops into Iraq in 1923.

1922

Gloster Nightjar
Carrier-based biplane fighter, modified from the Nieuport Nighthawk after Nieuport closed down and Gloster bought the rights. Some 22 went into service.

Blackburn R-1 Blackburn
Carrier-based biplane recon/spotter.

Blackburn T.2 Dart
Carrier-based torpedo bomber.

Gloster Grebe
RAF's first post WWI fighter.

Made out of wood, it was used in a variety of roles but was most famous for special operations raids into the heart of German territory

Produced by De Havilland Aircraft Company Ltd, the Mosquito was originally designed as an unarmed fast bomber. Nicknamed the Wooden Wonder, it was constructed of a variety of woods which produced a fuselage only needing seven balsawood/spruce bulkheads for reinforcement. Wings were made in one piece, mainly of spruce and plywood, and when assembled both the plywood-covered fuselage and wings were covered by a layer of doped fabric, which was allowed to dry before the aircraft's camouflage was

applied. Engines and major systems were then fitted and this method of construction resulted in one of the fastest aircraft in service with any air force and also made it very quick to build.

Operational service was both extensive and varied, the Mosquito seeing action as a fighter, fighter-bomber, light bomber and also undertaking roles such as photo-reconnaissance, anti-submarine warfare, attacks on shipping, nightfighter duties and operations with Pathfinder squadrons.

1924

Avro 549 Aldershot
iplane bomber originally designed to rop one large bomb. Subsequently hanged to four 500lb bombs externally

1924

Avro Andover
Only four built in two versions. Type 561 were flying ambulances, Type 563 was a 12-seater transport for the run between

Fairey Fawn
Light bomber/recon from the 1920s.

De Havilland Humming Bird
The DH.53 was used for comms/training.

Armstrong Whitworth Siskin
Aerobatic biplane fighter post WWI.

DE HAVILLAND DH.98 MOSQUITO B MK XVI

FACT BOX

TOP SPEED: 415mph
ARMAMENT: Mosquito bombers were unarmed. Fighters were fitted with: 4×20 mm (.79in) Hispano MkII cannon (fuselage) and four .303in Browning machine guns in the nose
BOMB LOAD: 4,000lb (Various types)
ENGINE: Two Rolls-Royce Merlin 76/77 liquid-cooled V12 engines, each producing 1,710hp, a total of 3420hp
NUMBER BUILT: 7,781 produced **DESIGNER:** Geoffrey de Havilland
SERVICE LIFE: July 1941 to January 1950

1924

Vickers Virginia
Biplane heavy bomber that served frontline units until 1938. After becoming obsolete as a bomber was used for photo recon and parachute training.

1924

Hawker Woodcock
Nightfighter with Vickers MG that fired through the propellor arc. Charles Lindbergh used one to fly from Paris to London after his spectacular solo trip.

Handley Page Hyderabad
H.P.24 heavy bomber introduced in 1925.

Supermarine Southampton
Most successful interwar flying boat.

Fairey Fox

AVRO LANCASTER

The iconic heavy bomber first flew in 1941 and was at the heart of Bomber Command's fight against Nazi Germany. You can still hear the roar of the Rolls-Royce Merlin engines at Battle of Britain events and airshows today

1927

Armstrong Whitworth Atlas
Designed for an Army co-operation role the Atlas was a single seater biplane that served at home and in Egypt. It was used for comms and as an advanced trainer.

1928

Beardmore Inflexible
Massive, experimental three-engined transport plane. It was made entirely from metal and had a wing span of 157ft but the engines were underpowered.

Bristol Type 105 Bulldog
Famous interwar biplane fighter.

De Havilland Gypsy Moth
One of a range of Moths from DH.

Hawker Fury
First biplane fighter to achieved 200mph.

Lancaster I PA474 of the Battle of Britain
Memorial Flight flies over the North Kent coast
in September 2011 (Jarrod Cotter)

VITAL STATS

TOP SPEED: 287mph **SERVICE CEILING:** 24,500ft
ARMAMENT: Eight 0.303in Browning machine-guns (defensive)
BOMB LOAD: 14,000lb **ENGINE:** Rolls-Royce Merlin x4
NUMBER BUILT: 7,373
DESIGNER: Roy Chadwick
SERVICE LIFE: December 1941 to October 1956

1932

De Havilland Tiger Moth
The DH.82 Tiger Moth was initially used
for training but also saw service in WWII
in maritime surveillance and defensive
patrols against invasion.

1933

Fairey Seal
Carrier-based recon spotter could be
launched from warships with a catapult.
Also used to fire torpedos and as a target
tug. Replaced by Swordfish in 1936.

Bolton Paul P.75 Overstrand
Last medium bomber biplane.

Gloster Gauntlet
Last open cockpit biplane fighter.

Hawker Hind
Interwar light biplane bomber.

THE LANCASTER IN FOCUS

The origins of the Lancaster can be traced back to 1936 when the RAF was looking to re-equip with up-to-date monoplane bombers. Air Ministry Specification P.13/36 for a so-called 'medium bomber' formed the basis of the design for Avro's twin-engined Manchester aeroplane.

However, the genesis of the Lancaster lay in the failure of the Manchester's twin Rolls-Royce Vulture engines to provide adequate performance. The Manchester was basically a sound fuselage let down by its powerplants. To remedy the design the wing was extended and four Rolls-Royce Merlin engines were fitted. The resulting successful configuration was initially called the Manchester III, but was later renamed as the Lancaster.

The prototype Lancaster, BT308, made its first flight on 9 January 1941. The first production machine, L7527, flew on 31 October 1941. Its performance was simply outstanding and large-scale production soon began at several factories.

No.44 (Rhodesia) Squadron at RAF Waddington, Lincolnshire, became the first unit to receive Lancasters on Christmas Eve 1941 when three aircraft arrived. However,

1. The Lancaster prototype BT308 which made its first flight on 9 January 1941 (Air Ministry)
2. A staged picture with 'V' for victory lights highlighting the Lancaster's importance during World War II (British Official)
3. The bomb load most commonly used for area bombing raids, which was termed 'Usual' (British Official)

it was not until 3 March 1942 that the Lancaster entered actual operational service when four bombers from No.44 Squadron set off for Heligoland Bight on a mine-laying operation.

The first night bombing operation with Lancasters took place on the night of 10/11 March 1942, when two 44 Squadron Lancasters participated in a raid on Essen. Many future raids by Lancasters would go on to make headline news, the first of which was the daylight bombing of the MAN Diesel factory at Augsburg in southern Germany on 17 April 1942. On that raid Sqn Ldr J.D. Nettleton became the first of ten Lancaster aircrew to be awarded the Victoria Cross.

Lancasters participated in the first 'Thousand Bomber' raid on the night of

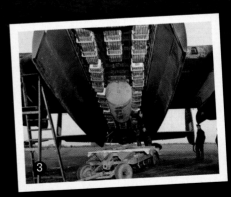

1936

Fairey Swordfish
Biplane torpedo bomber that achieved spectacular success against Italian navy and saw action against the **Bismarck**. Remained in front line service until VE Day.

1937

Fairey Battle
Light bomber with three man crew was slow and limited in range. Was used in early WWII but crippling losses meant it was withdrawn by the end of 1940.

Bristol Blenheim
Light bomber and long range fighter.

Gloster Gladiator
Last biplane fighter for the RAF.

Handley Page Harrow
Heavy bomber used as transporter in WWII.

The raid was a success, with the Möhne and Eder dams both being breached

30/31 May 1942. Codenamed Operation *Millennium*, a total of 1,047 bombers were despatched to Cologne.

On the clear moonlit night of 16/17 May 1943 the newly formed 617 Squadron successfully carried out what became the most single famous operation in the history of aerial warfare. The Squadron, commanded by Wing Commander Guy Gibson, set out to destroy key dams in the industrial heartland of Germany on Operation Chastise, better known as the Dam Busters raid. For the attack the squadron used a special weapon codenamed Upkeep, and actually termed a mine but more commonly referred to as the 'bouncing bomb'.

The Lancasters used for the raid were B.III (Specials), modified to be able to carry one Upkeep each in a specially designed calliper device that could rotate it at the 500rpm required for the weapon to bounce off the surface of the water. Furthermore, the bomb needed to be dropped from just 60ft, at night, and at a specified speed and exact distance from the dam.

The raid was a success, with the Möhne and Eder dams both being breached and the Sorpe damaged. Of the 16 Lancasters that reached their targets eight were lost, with only three of the 56 aircrew surviving being shot down. It was for this daring operation that Gibson was awarded the Victoria Cross.

Lancasters not only made a vital and hugely significant contribution to Bomber Command's night offensive, but they also helped to turn the tide in the major land battles of 1944 by bombing the German army in the field and flying tactical sorties aimed at precision targets.

At the end of the war Lancasters carried out two humanitarian operations. Operation *Manna* came before the German surrender and saw Lancasters dropping food to the starving Dutch population. When the war was over they flew many sorties on Operation *Exodus*, which was the repatriation of liberated Allied prisoners of war back to England.

During the course of World War II Lancasters had carried out around 156,000 sorties and dropped approximately 608,612 tons of high explosives.

After the war a number of Bomber Command squadrons continued to be equipped with the Lancaster, until the type was replaced by the Avro Lincoln. The last bomber unit to operated Lancasters, No. 49 Squadron, converted to Lincolns in March 1950.

With the departure of the lend-lease Liberators after the war, the Lancaster became the principal land-based maritime reconnaissance aircraft used by Coastal Command. The last example of the type to be operated in service was Lancaster MR.3 RF325, which was used by the School of Maritime Reconnaissance at RAF St Mawgan in Cornwall and was retired with a farewell ceremony on 15 October 1956, bringing to a close its illustrious career.

The Lancaster's importance to the war effort was ideally summed up by Air Chief Marshal Sir Arthur Harris in December 1945, "I believe that the Lancaster was the greatest single factor in winning the war."

1. A typical Lancaster squadron photograph. This is No. 101 Squadron (Crown Copyright) **2.** The bomb load used for industrial demolition, which was termed 'Abnormal' (British Official) **3.** A typical photograph from a Lancaster bombing raid, taken on the night of 18/19 April 1944 (Crown Copyright)

1937

Hawker Hurricane
Accounted for 60% of victories in Battle of Britain and served in all major theatres of WWII as fighter and ground support. Rugged and could take a lot of punishment.

1938

Handley Page Hampden
Twin-engined medium bomber served in early war missions over Europe but was withdrawn by Bomber Command by late 1942. Cramped conditions for crew

Blackburn Skua
Two-man, carrier-based dive bomber.

Short Sunderland
The S.25 flying boat patrol bomber.

Vickers Wellington
Early war long-range medium bomber

GLOSTER METEOR

The RAF's first jet fighter saw service intercepting V1 flying bombs and was used in a variety of roles at home and in air forces around the world

As the RAF's first operational jet fighter, the Meteor saw action during World War II and later, during the Korean War. Initially powered by Sir Frank Whittle's new jet engines, the Meteor flew for the first time in March 1943. It was soon used to intercept Nazi V1 flying bombs and later excelled as a fighter, night fighter, ground attack aircraft, photo-reconnaissance plane and jet trainer.

The Meteor was widely exported and saw service all over the world with the RAF and Fleet Air Arm, the Australian Air Force, the Belgian, Argentine, Brazilian and the Israeli Air Forces.

While the Meteor was not the most sophisticated jet fighter, quickly surpassed by more modern Soviet and American designs with better airframes, its formidable armament and robust design meant it served admirably as the RAF's workhorse during the early years of the Cold War.

VITAL STATS

TOP SPEED: 600mph
ARMAMENT:
4×20mm British Hispano MkV cannons
3in or 5in rockets
BOMB LOAD: Two 1,000lb bombs
ENGINE: Two Rolls-Royce Derwent 8 Turbojets
NUMBER BUILT: 3,947

1939

Supermarine Spitfire
The most famous fighter of all time. Fast, agile it underwent numerous upgrades and versions throughout the war and was the main weapon against the Luftwaffe

1939

Bolton Paul Defiant
No forward firing guns, used a rear turret to shoot down enemy bombers but was vulnerable to Bf 109s. Eventually replaced by Mosquito and Beaufighter

Blackburn B.26 Botha
Four seater recon/torpedo bomber

De Havilland Flamingo
Airliner used for transport and comms.

Hawker Henley
Two seater target tug based on Hurricane

1940

Bristol Type 156 Beaufighter
Initially used as a night fighter interceptor,
it could house radar and heavy armament.
Went on to use rockets in ground attacks
and torpedos against shipping.

1940

Handley Page Halifax
Heavy bomber served throughout WWII.
Upgraded versions added better engines,
increased payload and revised defensive
turret. Used by Commonwealth countries

Douglas Boston
Light bomber/recon. Night fighter - Havoc

Fairey Albacore
Carrier-based torpedo bomber biplane.

Avro Manchester
Failed forerunner to the Lancaster.

BAE HARRIER GR7/GR9

The Harrier Jump Jet was the first operational VTOL (Vertical Take Off and Landing) aircraft in the world and proved itself in air combat during the Falklands War

The Harrier was originally conceived to operate from hidden locations in the forests of West Germany to counter the threat of invasion from the USSR. It soon became apparent that this most versatile of aircraft could be used for many more roles than was first intended. The Sea Harrier was a variant designed to provide air defence for Royal Navy task groups. The first generation GR.1/GR.3 Harriers were developed by Hawker Siddeley while the second generation GR5/GR7/GR9 were redeveloped by McDonnell Douglas and British Aerospace.

In service with the RAF in multi-role operations, the iconic Harrier of the Falklands Conflict is one of very few foreign designed military aircraft produced under license in the USA. The US Marine Corps continues to fly the AV-8B Harrier II Plus today with plans to do so until 2030 although the last GR9 Harrier was retired from RAF service in 2010.

1940

Curtiss P-36 Hawk
American fighter that served with Commonwealth forces, including the RAF over Burma, and also Axis countries who used captured stocks.

1940

Curtiss P-40 Tomahawk
Was based on the P-36 and used by most Allied countries in WWII. Later versions known as Kittyhawk. Used extensively in the Middle East and North Africa.

Short Stirling
First four engine heavy bomber of WWII.

Martin Baltimore
US light bomber supplied as Lend-Lease.

Boeing B-17 Flying Fortress
US heavy bomber used in 1941 by RAF.

(Staff Sgt. Aaron Allmon)

HARRIER GR7/7A GR9 GR9A Specifications

TOP SPEED: 1,065kph (661mph)
SERVICE CEILING: 50,000ft (15,170m)
MAX RANGE: 5,382km (3,310 miles with 4 x drop tanks)
ARMAMENT: 2 x 30mm Aden cannons, 4 x wing weapon pylons, 4 x LAU-5003 rocket pods (19 x CRV7 70mm rockets each) or 4 x Matra rocket pods (18 x SNEB 68mm rockets each) or 6 x AIM-9 Sidewinder missiles or 4 x AGM-65 Maverick missiles.
BOMB LOAD: The Paveway series of laser-guided bombs or unguided iron bombs
ENGINE: GR7/9 - 1 x Rolls-Royce Pegasus Mk. 105 vectored thrust turbofan, 21,750lb (96.7kN)
NUMBER BUILT: 72 Harrier II
DESIGNER: Based on the Kestrel design by Sir Sydney Camm, Ralph Hooper of Hawker Aircraft, and Stanley Hooker (later Sir Stanley Hooker) of the Bristol Engine Company **RAF SERVICE LIFE:** 1990 to 2010

1941

De Havilland Mosquito
Twin engine multi-role fighter bomber made almost entirely from wood. In 1941 was one of the fastest aircraft in the world and was used as a nightfighter from 1942.

1941

Hawker Typhoon
Fighter-bomber originally designed to replace Hurricane but was plagued with problems. From 1943 ground attack rockets were added.

Consolidated B-24 Liberator
US long range bomber used as transporter.

Northrop N-3PB
Served with Norwegian unit of RAF.

Brewster SB2A Buccaneer
Awful scout/bomber used as target tug.

THE HARRIER II IN FOCUS

Harrier development began in 1957 when Sir Sydney Camm, Ralph Hooper of Hawker Aviation and Sir Stanley Hooker of the Bristol Engine Company met to consider the potential combination of the existing Olympus and Orpheus jet engines into a power plant capable of producing direct-able thrust. Thus the Pegasus engine was conceived and developed. It was however, the Hawker company which can be credited with the initial idea of using the Pegasus to meet a NATO specification for a light tactical-support fighter that would eventually evolve into the Harrier Jump Jet. The Hawker Company then decided to fund the construction of two prototypes - designated the P1127. The first - XP831 - was completed in July 1960 and immediately commenced static testing followed by its first tethered flight when the new Pegasus engine became available in October of the same year. Conventional take-off was first achieved on 7 July 1961 culminating in the

first ever transition from VTOL flight to level flight by a transonic aircraft on the 8th of September of the same year.

Several further development stages resulted in the Kestrel FGA.1 which first flew on 7 March 1964 of which nine examples were constructed. A special 'Tripartate' squadron was formed to evaluate the new marque consisting of British, American and German pilots based at RAF West Raynham in Norfolk. During the evaluation one of the test aircraft was lost and on completion of this stage of testing the remaining eight were then transferred to the USA for further evaluation. With the testing considered a success by 1966 the RAF had ordered 60 production aircraft based on the upgraded P1127 design and service designated - Harrier GR.1.

The GR.1 was soon followed by the GR.1A featuring the upgraded Pegasus 102

engine which was then replaced by the GR.3 variant with the Pegasus 103 power-plant and a new avionics suite giving it the new, distinctive, nose profile. A total of 114 GR.1s were delivered including the T.2, T.2A and T.4 two-seat trainer variants, which were also fully combat capable. Many existing GR.1s were also then upgraded to GR.3 standard with further examples being newly manufactured. This production run of the GR.3 version was finally completed by the early 1980s. The GR.3 was the RAF Harrier version to see action in the Falklands Conflict, primarily in the ground attack role.

Later in the 1980s after the lessons of the Falklands, the Harrier saw further development as a joint venture between British Aerospace and McDonnell Douglas. The new aircraft featured a raised cockpit for better all-round visibility, with revised engine configuration and improved

1942

Douglas Dakota
US designed military transport aircraft, developed from DC-3 airliner. One variant used to drop paratroops in invasion of Sicily. Sent to Britain under Lend-Lease.

1942

Avro Lancaster
Iconic British heavy bomber excelled as night bomber and day time precision raids. Late war versions carried largest payload of any WWII bomber.

Airspeed AS.51 Horsa
Troop-carrying glider for 30 men.

Martin B-26 Marauder
US bomber used by RAF and South Africa.

North American P-51 Mustang
Fighter bomber used in many theatres.

1. A Joint Force Harrier jet is pictured high over RAF Akrotiri in Cyprus shortly before the iconic aircraft was decommissioned (Luis Holden)

avionics. The most significant improvement to the airframe being the use of composites in a new one-piece wing, therefore reducing the aircraft's overall weight and increasing its weapons payload capacity. The RAF initially took delivery of the new Harrier II GR5 in 1990 which then progressed to the GR7 in 1992 and GR7a in 1998. Then came the final Harrier development iterations - the GR9 and GR9a in 2006. Following the development of the Harrier II GR5, all remaining previous models have been upgraded to the new specifications and have thus been updated within this timeline due to being built on the same basic airframe.

Due to the extended range capability of the Harrier II making it suitable for the interdiction role the first combat deployment of the redesigned aircraft occurred after the first Gulf War in 1993 where several were assigned to patrol the no-fly zone in Iraq.

Following this the Harrier II delivered its first combat strikes during the Bosnian crisis in the Yugoslavian civil war in 1995. Harrier II's flew approximately 126 ground attack missions during the conflict using laser guided pathfinder munitions, often being target-designated by accompanying RAF Sepecat Jaguar aircraft. Following the 1998 Defence Review, Harrier II's of the RAF and the Fleet Air Arm were then both managed by Joint Force Harrier Command (JCF) based at RAF Cottesmore.

During the Kosovo Crisis of 1999 12 RAF Harrier II's taking part in Operation *Allied Force* carried out 870 sorties during the 78 day bombing campaign with no casualties. Then, in the second Gulf War of 2003, during Operation *Telic,* RAF Harrier II's hunted for Iraqi Scud missile launchers. The provided close air support for the troops throughout the conflict and during the Battle of Basra destroyed ground installations and enemy vehicles. The final operational deployment of the Harrier II was in the ongoing conflict in Afghanistan beginning in 2004 with the deployment of 6 Harrier II GR7s to Kandahar airbase where the last combat loss of a Harrier occurred when the Taliban destroyed one on the ground with an RPG rocket. In 2007 the GR7s were rotated out of service at Kandahar in favour of upgraded GR9s which were finally withdrawn from the Afghan theatre in June 2009, having flown for over 22,000 hours over 8,500 sorties.

On the 19th October 2010 it was announced in the Strategic Defence and Security Review that the Harrier II was to be retired by April 2011 in a controversial move which would strip a vital capability from the RAF with no suitable replacement available in the form of the F35 for some time. The last Harrier II GR9s left RAF service on 15 December 2010 with the remaining 72 airframes being disposed of as a source of spares for operational USMC Harrier IIs for £116 million, significantly less than the original purchase cost of one airframe.

2. Hawker Siddeley Harrier GR.1 configured for the ground attack role during the 1970s **3.** A Royal Air Force Harrier GR.3 aircraft of No. 233 OCU hovers with landing gear down during Air Fete '84 at RAF Mildenhall, Suffolk (TSgt Jose Lopez Jr., USAF) **4.** British Aerospace RAF Harrier II GR5 transitioning from hover mode into forward flight (Anthony Noble) **5.** A Harrier GR7A in flight over the mountain ranges in Afghanistan during a mission in 2004 (Wg Cdr Bruce Hedley) **6.** A Harrier GR9 from IV Squadron, RAF Cottesmore is pictured during a sortie over Afghanistan in 2008. Paveway IV laser guided bombs can be seen on the outermost pylon underneath the wings (Crown Copyright)

The Handley Page Victor
Ignihilita quidestiusam nimaior as possimpor ma niminci issitem volenis et entiisc ipienit, od maximus, nonsequis es ducionima conet accus placcab ium fugia

The Handley Page Victor
Ignihilita quidestiusam nimaior as possimpor ma niminci issitem volenis et entiisc ipienit, od maximus, nonsequis es ducionima conet accus placcab ium fugia

The Handley Page Victor
Ignihilita quidestiusam nimaior as possim

The Handley Page Victor
Ignihilita quidestiusam nimaior as possim

The Handley Page Victor
Ignihilita quidestiusam nimaior as possim

AVRO VULCAN B.1

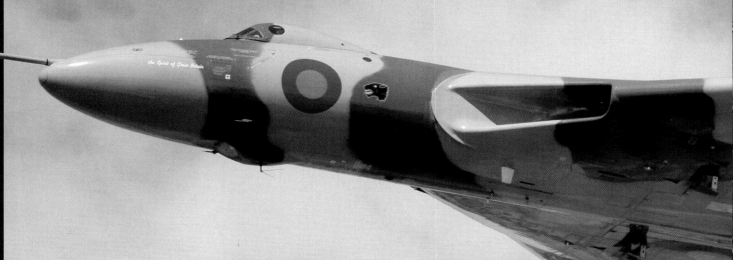

A stalwart of the Cold War era, the Vulcan was a massive bomber and part of the strategic nuclear strike force

The Vulcan was one of three V-class aircraft known as the United Kingdom's strategic nuclear strike force (or V-force) alongside the Vickers Valiant and the Handley Page Victor. In 1956, answering the Air Ministry's call for a nuclear-capable bomber with exceptional range, Avro delivered the Vulcan B.1 – the world's first jet-powered high-altitude bomber with a delta wing configuration.

The distinctive swept-back wing granted manoeuvrability, enormous lift and a low radar profile. The B.2 followed, with improved engines and systems. By 1962 the RAF could scramble two Vulcans, each with a five-man crew, from any nuclear-weapon carrying RAF base in the UK. Atomic or conventional bombs could be deployed to major Soviet targets from 55,000ft.

The aircraft was a centrepiece of the UK's nuclear deterrent until 1969. By 1982 the RAF had withdrawn the Vulcan as a weapons platform, with six repurposed for aerial refuelling. It was officially retired in 1984.

1943

Fairey Barracuda
Carrier-based torpedo and dive bomber made entirely from metal. Intended as a replacement for the Swordfish was used in the attack on the **Tirpitz**.

1943

Supermarine Sea Otter
Flying boat development of the Walrus and was the last biplane to enter service with the RN and RAF. Used for air-sea rescue and recon patrols.

Vickers Warwick
Large plane mainly used for transport.

Avro York
Transport plane derived from the Lancaster.

Bristol Type 163 Buckingham
Originally a bomber, used for transport.

VITAL STATS

TOP SPEED: 645mph at altitude (B.1)
ARMAMENT: Bomb load only (B.1) / x1 Blue Steel missile (B.2)
Bomb load: 1 nuclear bomb (free-fall) or 21 1,000lb conventional bombs
ENGINE: Four Bristol Olympus 101, or 102 or 104 Turbojet (B.1) / four Bristol
Siddeley Olympus 200-series, or 301 **NUMBER BUILT:** 136
DESIGNER: Stuart Duncan Davies **SERVICE LIFE:** 1956 to 1984

1944

Gloster Meteor
First British jet fighter and only Allied
aircraft to undertake combat operations.
Was one of few planes fast enough to
catch V1 bombs and destroy them.

1944

Hawker Tempest
Originally an improved version of the
Typhoon working better at high altitude
but received own designation. Used as
inte... bombers, dett...

De Havilland Hornet
Successor to Mosquito, served in Far East.

Avro 691 Lancastrian
Passenger and mail transporter.

Avro Type 694 Lincoln

PANAVIA TORNADO

A stalwart of the RAF for the last 30 years, the Tornado has filled numerous roles

The Panavia Tornado is a variable geometry, two-seat, day or night, all weather strike aircraft which has been the backbone of RAF offensive operations for several decades now. The prototype first flew on 14 August 1974 and the first operational Tornado GR.1s were delivered to No. IX (B) Squadron at Honington in January 1982. The Tornado is capable of delivering a wide range of weapons and can fly automatically at low-level using terrain-following radar. By using its forward-looking infrared systems and pilot's night-vision goggles it's a very capable platform for night-time operations. It has been in service with the RAF for more than 30 years now, although a combination of major upgrade programmes and numerous continual enhancements has kept the aircraft amongst the forefront of all attack aircraft. It is presently expected that the Tornado will be retired in 2019.

1946

De Havilland Vampire
Early jet fighter with distinctive twin boom configuration. It was the second jet fighter, after the Meteor, and replaced most piston-engine war time planes.

1951

English Electric Canberra
Jet-powered fast bomber successor to the Mosquito. Outstanding high altitude performance meant it served as an early tactical nuclear strike aircraft.

Avro Shackleton
Long range maritime patrol craft.

De Havilland Venom
Fighter bomber derived from Vampire.

Hawker Hunter
Jet interceptor set air speed record in 1953.

(RAF/Crown Copyright)

TORNADO GR.4

TOP SPEED: 997mph
ARMAMENT: Mauser 27mm cannon
Bomb/missile load: Storm Shadow, Brimstone, ALARM, AIM-9L, Paveway II or III, EPW II or III, Paveway IV, BL755
ENGINE: Two Turbo Union RB199 turbofans
NUMBER BUILT: 218 **SERVICE LIFE:** January 1982 to c.2019

1955

Vickers Valiant
Four jet, high-altitude bomber and once part of the V-Force. It has the distinction of being the only V-Force bomber to have dropped live nuclear weapons.

1956

Gloster Javelin
Night and all-weather dual engine interceptor that was a successor to the Meteor. Served alongside the Lightning which outperformed it.

Handley Page Victor
Third member of nucear V-Force.

Avro Vulcan
Huge bomber and also V-Force member.

Scottish Aviation Twin Pioneer
Civilian and military STOL transporter.

VITAL STATS

TOP SPEED: 1381mph
ALTITUDE CEILING: 55,000ft
ARMAMENT (STANDARD): Mauser 27mm Cannon
ARMAMENT (VARIABLE) INCLUDES: AMRAAM, ASRAAM, Meteor BVRAAM, Storm Shadow, ALARM, AIM-9 Sidewinder
BOMB LOAD (VARIABLE) INCLUDES: Enhanced Paveway II, Paveway IV laser-guided bombs, JDAM, 1000lb freefall class
ENGINE: Two Eurojet EJ200 turbojets
NUMBER BUILT: Over 500 to date
SERVICE LIFE: 2003 to present

1959

English Electric Lightning

A giant leap forward in jet-powered interceptors, designed to catch high altitude Soviet nuclear bombers. It served for two decades and was incredibly fast.

1962

Folland Gnat

Compact light fighter was ordered by the RAF for use as a trainer. Famously, it went on to be used for many years by the Red Arrows aerobatic team.

Hawker Siddeley Kestrel

Experimental aircraft that led to the Harrier.

Westland Wessex

Search and rescue helicopter.

Lockheed C-130 Hercules

Turboprop military transport aircraft.

EUROFIGHTER TYPHOON

The Typhoon is the RAF's most advanced multi-role combat aircraft. Since its introduction in 2003 it has been instrumental in air-policing, support missions, and high-intensity conflict around the world

1969

Hawker Siddeley Harrier
The original GR.1 Harrier was designed to operate away from airbases in West Germany to counter a Soviet invasion. The fighter had V/STOL capability.

1969

Blackburn Buccaneer
Entered Navy service in 1962 as a carrier strike plane. Bought by the MoD for the RAF in 1969 as cheap alternative when the BAC TSR-2 was cancelled.

McDonnell Douglas Phantom
British F-4K version for interceptor role.

Hawker Siddeley Nimrod
Early warning platform, eventually canned.

Scottish Aviation Bulldog
T1 model used as basic trainer by RAF.

THE EUROFIGHTER IN FOCUS

1. The 2013 RAF solo Typhoon display is carried out by 29(R) Sqn based at RAF Conningsby (Alan Wilson) **2.** Air-to-air ASRAAM missiles fitted to a Royal Air Force Typhoon fighter jet (Geoff Lee/MOD) **3.** 3(F) Squadron RAF Eurofighter Typhoon based at RAF Coningsby, Lincoln, England firing an ASRAAM missile

Typhoon is a fifth-generation jet fighter that entered RAF service in 2003. Initially designed to secure air superiority it has evolved to carry out Close Air Support, Maritime Attack, Suppression of Enemy Air Defence, and Deep Air Support roles. It is manufactured by Eurofighter Jagdflugzeug GmbH, a multinational company formed in 1986. The Eurofighter Typhoon's core strength is its agility and effectiveness as a dog-fighter in air-to-air conflict. Just 15% of its surface is metal, with lightweight composite materials delivering a strong airframe while maintaining a low radar profile. It is now equipped to take on air-to-surface missions, with capacity for up to six bombs and six missiles, plus a cannon and a targeting pod. The latest upgradable sensor, navigation and control systems give the pilot optimum combat capability in both beyond-visual-range and close combat. The key to the jet's operational flexibility is its mission-variable weapon load. The growing list of compatible armaments and equipment has been expanded through production revisions. It supports enhanced Paveway laser-guided bombs, Storm Shadow long range missiles, and the RAFs Brimstone radar-guided missiles.

The full effectiveness of such an advanced fighter is only realised through speed and power. Eurofighter is driven by two Eurojet EJ200 engines providing a highly advantageous thrust-to-weight ratio. Each can produce 60kN (13,500lbf) of thrust, rising to more than 90kN with afterburners. It can also achieve a supersonic speed of Mach 1.5 without the use of afterburners – known as supercruise. Incredibly, precision guided weapons can actually be launched at this speed, extending its ability to deliver military air power.

The development of the Eurofighter Typhoon started back in 1983 as a collaboration between the UK, Germany, France, Italy and Spain. By 1986 British Aerospace had test-flown a demonstration aircraft. BAE Systems, Airbus, and Leonardo S.p.A then formed Eurofighter Jagdflugzeug GmbH to oversee design, production and upgrades. A multitude of revisions later and the first prototype aircraft – sporting a 'DA' (Development Aircraft) designation – successfully flew on 27 March 1994. In September 1998 the aircraft was named Typhoon and the first production contracts were signed.

Production was divided into three tranches, each designed to modify its capabilities in-line with operational needs. The RAF took their first Eurofighter delivery in 2003 for development and testing purposes, with activation of the first Typhoon Squadron at RAF Coningsby in 2005. Since then it has been involved in high-profile operations and missions, such as Libya in 2011. Ten Eurofighters were deployed there for combat and reconnaissance, clocking up an impressive 4,500 flying hours without the need for a single engine change. Since 2015 the aircraft has flown more than 900 missions over Iraq and Syria to support international forces against Islamic State and most recently worked alongside the Romanian Air Force to defend NATOs airspace over the Black Sea.

The UK government recently extended the life of the first Typhoons to 2040, with two additional RAF front-line squadrons to give a total of seven. As of June 2017 the UK has ordered over 230 Typhoons with 145 delivered and in operation.

By 2015 the estimated cost of the Typhoon programme had surpassed £17.6 billion, with the price of each aircraft a staggering £125 million – making it easily one of the most expensive weapon systems in RAF history.

1974

SEPECAT Jaguar
Anglo-French close air support attack aircraft capable of nuclear strikes. Served with the RAF until 2007 when it was replaced by the Tornado and Eurofighter.

1976

Hawker Siddeley Hawk
Advanced trainer originally produced by Hawker Siddeley and then by BAE. Used by the Red Arrows display team and still in production in UK and India.

Westland Sea King
Versatile search and rescue helicopter.

Panavia Tornado
Mainstay of British combat aircraft.

Boeing Chinook
Heavy lift transport saw action in Falklands.

4. A RAF Typhoon pilot enters the cockpit as the sun sets over Gioia del Colle, southern Italy (Sgt Pete Mobbs/MOD) **5.** Eurofighter airframe used for testing on display at Piet Smedts Aero, Baarlo, The Netherlands **6.** A pilot from 29 Reserve Squadron disembarks from his Typhoon aircraft at RAF Coningsby, Lincolnshire (SAC Daniel Herrick LBIPP/MOD) **7.** Typhoon pilot arrives in Albacete Air Force Base, Spain during exercises in 2015 (Allied Joint Force Command Brunssum) **8.** Eurofighter Typhoon DA4 built 1997 as a development and test aircraft on display at Imperial War Museum, Duxford (Alan Wilson)

4

5

6

7

8

1989

BAE Harrier II
The second version of the V/STOL aircraft designated GR5, GR7 and GR9. Served in Kosovo, Iraq and Afghanistan as close support and air interdiction fighter.

1990

Boeing E-3 Sentry
Commonly known as AWACS, the airborne early warning and control aircraft is known for the rotating radar dome and served in Operation **Desert Storm**.

Augusta-Westland Merlin
Joint-production, medium lift helicopter.

Eurofighter Typhoon
The current state-of-the-art fighter.

Airbus A400M Atlas
Multi-national turboprop military transport

RAF BIGGIN HILL

The iconic base was the heart of the fight against the Luftwaffe in the Battle of Britain

Today, perched on the top of the North Downs in Bromley, lies London Biggin Hill Airport – formerly RAF Biggin Hill. Best known for its key role as a fighter station and strategic airfield in the Battle of Britain, the base gained the nickname, The Strongest Link, due to its invaluable defence of London and southeast England from German bombers during both WWI and WWII. Sited 600ft above sea level and only 14 miles from Central London, Biggin Hill was ideally placed to control the sector as Fighter Command for No.11 Group. However, that prominence also made it a prime target for the Luftwaffe, with repeated attacks that would see several buildings destroyed and personnel killed. Despite the

best efforts of Hermann Göring's bomber units to destroy the base during the Battle of Britain, RAF Biggin Hill continued to function as a strategic airfield, launching squadrons of Spitfires and Hurricanes that would ultimately claim hundreds of enemy aircraft and secure its reputation as the strongest link in the RAFs chain of airfields defending the UK.

RAF Biggin Hill

YEAR OPENED: 1918 (RAF)
YEAR CLOSED: 1992 (RAF)
STATION COMMANDER (BOB):
Group Captain Richard 'Dickie' Grice
SQUADRONS (BOB):
32, 64, 72, 74, 79, 92, 141, 610

1. Aerial view of London Biggin Hill Airport 2. Ground crew loading belts of ammunition for the guns of a Spitfire Mk I 3. The entrance to the RAF Station in the mid 1930s 4. Post-war, jets such as the Gloster Meteor appeared alongside the piston-engine aircraft 5. The plaque outside the airfield, commemorating the contribution it made to the war

Early Development

Having been requisitioned by the War Office in 1916, the airfield initially conducted the development and experimentation of wireless technology, including what would become air-to-air telephony and Radio Direction Finding (RDF). Experiments in the acoustic detection of aircraft carried out at Biggin Hill would lead to effective interception of German planes in the short years to come. This system was the precursor to radar, the invention of which was still more than a decade away.

In 1917 the Royal Flying Corp moved to Biggin Hill from its HQ at Joyce Green – the latter being prone to poor visibility due to mist from the Thames. The RFC then established the base as part of the London Air Defence Area, utilising a field at the adjacent Cudham Lodge Farm as a runway for 141 Squadron and their Bristol Fighter planes. Next to the airfield new hangars

The airfield initially conducted the development of wireless technology

and various ground buildings were erected. The RFCs move to the expanded facilities enabled protection of the region against attacks from Zeppelins, and Gotha and Staaken bombers. Meanwhile, inspired locals began referring to the base as, "Biggin on the Bump," due to its elevation in the nearby hills. By the end of April 1918 the RFC was no-more, replaced by Lord Trenchard's newly formed Royal Air

Force. The base would now be known by its official (albeit less colourful) name of RAF Biggin Hill.

After WWI the base returned to its former role as home to various experimental units working on anti-aircraft technology and innovations such as cockpit instrumentation. Fully realising the strategic value of the location of the base throughout World War I, RAF Biggin Hill closed down in 1929 for much-needed reconstruction and expansion work. New aircraft hangars were constructed, administrative buildings were expanded, blocks for technical work and even staff quarters and domestic living areas were built. The remodelling of the base was completed by 1932, with much of the original WWI-era structures flattened to make way.

But the work didn't stop there. By the late '30s Europe was once again in the grip of political unrest and rising hostilities. With the ascendency of the Nazi party and Hitler's ambitions becoming all too clear, there was little reason for the British to slow development of its airfields and bases. In 1938 yet more hangars, married quarters, mess halls and workshops were constructed, coinciding with the arrival of the base's first Hawker Hurricane fighters. Despite the expansion of the base over the previous two decades, it still maintained a grass runway – far too soft for the new fighters. London construction and civil engineering company Wimpey was contracted to carry out the work, owing to their track-record with the Air Ministry. A 4800ft tarmacadam runway was laid to support the weight of the new state-of-the-art Hurricanes.

The certainty of an impending war with Germany led to the construction of air raid shelters and buildings were camouflaged, including the planting of trees. Alongside sandbags and other reinforcements, the runway was toned-down to reduce its visibility from the air. Ground defence units were moved in, accompanied by anti-aircraft 'ack-ack' guns. Upon the outbreak of WWII on 3 September 1939, all civilians were ordered to leave the base.

The War Years

Shortly after the declaration of WWII, the RAF divided Great Britain's airspace into four Fighter Command Groups with RAF Biggin Hill designated as a Sector Station – a control hub for Sector C and squadrons of No. 11 Group. Using the designated radio call sign 'TOPHAT', Biggin Hill's Sector Control Room now commanded RAF Hawkinge in Kent, RAF Friston close to Beachey Head, and satellite airfields at Gravesend and West Malling.

No. 11 Group was under the command of Air Vice Marshall Keith Park who was able to strategically scramble and coordinate his squadrons via the Group Operations Room in a bunker at RAF Uxbridge. On the ground at Biggin Hill was Station Commander Group Captain Richard 'Dickie' Grice. As a decorated World War I fighter pilot, Grice was no stranger to attacks from German fighters and bombers. The acoustic detection technology first pioneered at Biggin Hill had since been superseded by radar, with stations placed all around the coast. Fighter Command could map enemy locations and pass this vital information through Group Headquarters to each Sector Control station.

Squadrons 32 and 79 were based at RAF Biggin Hill – both now flying the new Hurricanes. But with the outbreak of hostilities they were soon joined by No. 601 (County of London) flying twin-engine Bristol Blenheims. In May 1940 the Battle of France swiftly developed into the defence and evacuation of thousands of troops from Dunkirk. Activity to and from the base was at an all-time high. No. 242 Squadron arrived under Squadron Leader Douglas Bader. Bader, who had lost both his legs in an air-crash in 1931, had defied his injuries and returned to the RAF as a fighter pilot. He would go on to win scores of victories during both Dunkirk and the Battle of Britain. Hurricane pilots from squadrons 213, 229 and 242 also arrived at RAF Biggin Hill to support the troops at Dunkirk. As the evacuation progressed, the base's fighter planes would engage the Luftwaffe over the English Channel and provide cover for evacuee ships heading for Dover. Over 300,000 men made it home.

In early 1940, as the Battle of Britain approached, new air raid shelters were built at Biggin Hill and a concrete runway constructed. At the battle progressed, the base became a Spitfire station and was assigned several more squadrons – including numbers 72, 74 (Tiger Squadron), 92 (East India) and 610 (County of Chester) Auxiliary Squadron. These preparations would shortly prove invaluable. RAF Biggin Hill, and indeed the whole of Fighter Command, had caught the eye of the German High Command which now considered it a

1. Eight Royal Air Force Supermarine Spitfire Mk IX of No. 611 Squadron, based at RAF Biggin Hill, in 1943 **2.** Squadrons of Spitfires taking off from RAF Biggin Hill in 1942 **3.** Squadron Leader Edward 'Jack' Charles, commanding No 611 Squadron, chalks up the Biggin Hill Sector's 1,000th enemy aircraft, following a successful sweep over Normandy on 15 May 1943 **4.** St George's, the chapel at RAF Biggin Hill, in the 1960s **5.** The original WWII control tower at Biggin Hill **6.** The crew service the gun housing to make sure it's ready for operations against the Luftwaffe

priority target. On the 13 August 1940 the Germans planned their bomber raids on nine RAF airfields.

The Luftwaffe dispatched almost 2,000 aircraft to carry out massive attacks on RAF airfields in a bid for air-superiority. On 15 August the RAF scrambled around 150 Spitfires and Hurricanes into the skies above the south of England – the greatest number of fighter planes in the history of single operations up to that point. Every squadron in 11 Group was in the air with many being scrambled multiple times, including Biggin Hill's No. 32 Squadron. Despite overwhelming odds and the loss of 34 allied planes and 17 men, the RAF shot down 76 enemy aircraft and repelled wave after wave of attacks. The Germans named the day Black Thursday. Biggin Hill and Fighter Command had emerged victorious, but this victory would be short-lived.

On 19 August, 'The Hardest Day' arrived at Biggin Hill. Redoubling their efforts, this new German assault wave arrived from the English Channel. They were met in the

southeast by the fighters of 11 Group, but RAF Biggin Hill's elevated position south of the Thames placed it first in the firing line. Hundreds of bombs fell in the first few minutes alone, destroying several buildings and severely damaging the main runway. As ground staff rushed to repair the pot-holes, some of the largest air-to-air combat conflicts in history raged above them. Planes on the ground were blown up en-mass. Biggin Hill remained operational after hasty repairs, proving itself yet again as a stalwart contributor to the war effort.

The dust had barely settled when the Luftwaffe struck again. On Friday, 30 August it was, more than ever, intent on wiping RAF Biggin Hill from the map. Coastal radar stations detected almost 100 German planes over the English Channel. The first attacks hit the local area, but others hit radar stations on the coast. Without their early warning system, Fighter Command was rendered partially blind. A formation of nine Junkers bombers managed to avoid detection and, reaching the airfield, released their payload.

Workshops, the motor section, the WAAF's quarters and even the NAAFI were totally destroyed. A hangar and several aircraft inside were also demolished. Airmen and other personnel were killed or buried beneath rubble in direct hits to air-raid shelters. By the time the attack was over, Biggin Hill had lost 40 people. Under the ever-resilient leadership of Station Commander Grice, the survivors immediately began cleaning up the mess and restoring the almost unrecognisable base to an operational state.

The next day the Germans returned. This time the Operations Room was hit, severing

the link between the station and Fighter Command headquarters. Despite a runway littered with freshly-made craters, RAF Biggin Hill continued to successfully launch its fighters and no members of the RAF on the ground lost their lives. The base was only non-operational as a Sector Station for two hours.

Typifying British resourcefulness in the face of adversity, Group Captain Grice moved base Operations to a local shop in Biggin Hill village whilst repair work was carried out. Between August 1940 and January 1941, the airfield was attacked by the Luftwaffe twelve times, yet managed to remain operational throughout.

The Battle of Britain was over by the end of October 1940, and Germany's attacks shifted from RAF airfields to civilian and infrastructure targets in London – the Blitz had begun. Fighter Command now had time to recover and regroup, as did the exhausted pilots of 11 Group and its numerous bases. Biggin Hill scrambled its fighters to defend London, cementing its reputation as The Strongest Link in the RAFs chain of

airfields. The term was coined by Winston Churchill, in commending the airfield. The motto was incorporated into the Station's official crest in the form of a linked chain.

During 1941-42 the base saw an influx of new-variant Spitfires that would maintain air superiority in multiple operations for Fighter Command, including the raid on the German-occupied port of Dieppe (code-named Operation *Jubilee*). As the war progressed, squadrons from RAF Biggin Hill provided air support for various bombing offensives in Europe, escorting Lancasters and Halifaxes. The base maintained its active role as a Sector Station and airfield until the end of the war.

Following VE Day, squadrons based at Biggin Hill would be able to claim a total of 1,400 enemy aircraft destroyed in the course of WWII, with the loss of 453 Biggin Hill-based aircrew.

The Cold War and beyond

The Cold War ushered in a new period of relative calm for RAF Biggin Hill. The military conflict of WWII was swiftly replaced by economic and political conflict between the world's emerging superpowers. The base then saw a short period of use as a terminal by the RAFs Transport Command.

By the early '50s the base was home to regular and reserve fighter squadrons, including No. 168 (Royal Canadian Air Force). In 1951 Lord Dowding laid the foundation stone for a new memorial chapel to honour pilots who had lost their lives in the Battle of Britain. The chapel (which is still there today, its entrance flanked by replicas of a Spitfire and a Hurricane) was built on the site of one of the hangars destroyed by the Luftwaffe in 1940.

1952 saw the building of a new Air Traffic Control Tower. Gloster Meteor F4 jets became a common sight at the hangars, with the main runway extended in 1957 to accommodate the new Hawker Hunter F5 jets of No. 41 Squadron. However, the very nature of The Cold War led to Fighter Command diminishing as an organisation. The number of active squadrons were in decline, and increased jet travel from London's civil airports had constricted the available airspace. It was clear that The Cold War had no use for The Strongest Link at Biggin on the Bump.

By 1958 Biggin Hill's function as an operational station had ended. It did, however, become the Officer and Aircrew Selection Centre for the RAF, but by this time it was already a joint military and civilian airport. The airport was purchased by Orpington District Council in 1972.

The RAF finally left Biggin Hill in October 1992. It is now leased to Biggin Hill Airport Ltd which operates general aviation services and is home to commercial ventures, pilot training and historic flying clubs.

RAF UXBRIDGE

The famous home of No. 11 Group of RAF Fighter Command

1

2

RAF Uxbridge was in operation from 1917 to 2010, and during that time it was home to numerous units as well as acting as a depot. However, it is perhaps most famous for being the headquarters of No. 11 Group of Fighter Command, which was responsible for protecting London and the southeast of England throughout World War II. Although it is no longer an operational RAF station, it is home to the Battle of Britain Bunker, an underground operations room which now serves as a museum that is open to the public.

It all began when, in 1914, the London borough estate of Hillingdon House was put up for sale, and was purchased by the British Government the following year.

RAF Uxbridge

YEAR OPENED: 1917 (RFC)
YEAR CLOSED: 2010
SENIOR OPERATIONS OFFICER (BOB):
Wing Commander Willoughby de Broke
WWII RESPONSIBILITIES: Headquarters, Bomber Command (1936-1940); No. 11 Group (1936-1948); Headquarters No. 256 Win (23-28 April 1940); Headquarters 2nd Tactical Air Force (Feb-August 1944)

The original intention was to create a POW camp, but the local populations of Hillingdon and Uxbridge were outraged so the Government decided to build a military hospital instead. On 20 September 1915, the Canadian Convalescent Hospital

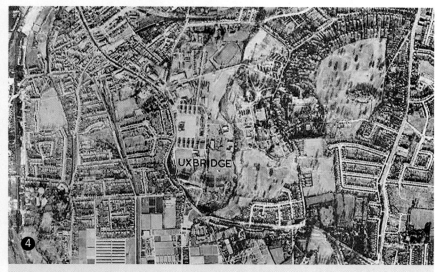

1. Telephonists of the WAAF at work at RAF Uxbridge in 1942 **2.** Douglas Bader was one of the famous faces to appear at Uxbridge. He convalesced there! after the accident which cost him his legs **3.** And after sorting out meals, the WAAF at Uxbridge set about entertaining with Leading Aircraftwoman Gladys Maugham, from East London, singing and tap dancing **4.** The site of the base, as seen from the air in 1945 **5.** Flight Lieutenant JG Eadie, Medical Officer at No. 11 Group HQ with part of his aircraft collection in April 1943

Area Medical Headquarters and Southern Area Barrack Stores, amongst others, were moved into Hillingdon House.

In 1925 a number of buildings were constructed around the edges of the parade ground, including a hospital for officers and an operations room. The following year, the Air Ministry selected the base to be the location for the Air Defence of Great Britain (ADGB), an RAF command that was staffed by both RAF and British Army personnel responsible for the air defence of the British Isles; it would be the precursor of RAF Fighter Command. The choice of RAF Uxbridge for ADGB was due to its short distance from the British Government and Whitehall.

RAF Uxbridge would see a number of now famous faces visiting and working in its grounds. One such person was Thomas Edward Lawrence, better remembered today as Lawrence of Arabia, who had enlisted in the RAF under the false name of John Hume-Ross. Here he undertook his basic training in the service in 1922, until being exposed for who he really was and forced to leave the following year.

Another person of note was Douglas Bader, who experienced a flying accident in 1931, which resulted in both his legs being amputated. Bader spent time at the hospital convalescing from his injuries the following year.

It would be on 1 May 1936 that No. 11 (Fighter) Group was established at RAF Uxbridge. Several months later, the ADGB was succeeded by RAF Fighter Command, and the headquarters of the command moved to Bentley Priory. However, elements of the ADGB remained to form RAF Bomber Command, which found headquarters in Hillingdon House.

Although only built just over a decade earlier, the operations room at RAF Uxbridge was found to be inadequate for No. 11 Group's needs; the buildings were made of wood, which became somewhat damp during the winter. As such, a new one was

opened, where wounded soldiers from France were sent to recover.

Later, during World War I, in November 1917, the armament school of the Royal Flying Corps (RFC) took up residence at Hillingdon House. Although the hospital remained in operation, there was some spare capacity which was made available to the RFC. The armaments school quickly established a number of firing ranges, which it used to instruct new recruits in the art of gunnery. It would not be long, however, before the hospital closed its doors. With the forming of the Royal Air Force on 1 April 1918, the station was transferred to the new service.

The next year, in 1919 RAF Uxbridge became home to the newly established No. 1 Depot in 1919, becoming a central depot for the RAF. Since the site was so large, it was decided to split it into two separate stations, the land on the eastern side of the Pinn River becoming known as RAF Hillingdon, while the remainder of the site retained the title RAF Uxbridge.

The station would grow during the inter-wars years, including the installation of a cinema, which was also utilised as a lecture theatre for new recruits. In late 1919, the RAF School of Music was moved to Uxbridge, while other units, such as the Headquarters Southern Area, the Southern

built in 1939, which was located about 60ft underground in order to offer it a degree of protection from enemy air attack. It was decided to retain the wooden operations rooms, which later became simply known as Building 76.

Following the outbreak of World War II, RAF Uxbridge was engaged in the movement of personnel between training units and operational squadrons fighting in France. In recent years, much recognition has been given to Polish pilots of the RAF, and it was at RAF Uxbridge that many of them were taught the ways of the service. During the subsequent Battle of Britain, No. 11 Group saw its number of personnel double, greatly expanding the number of men and women at the station. It would also be during 1940 that the RAF officer's hospital was transferred to the Women's Auxiliary Air Force (WAAF).

Another famous name to visit RAF Uxbridge was Prime Minister Winston Churchill, who arrived at the operations room on 16 August 1940 in order to witness how the Battle of Britain was handled by the RAF. It is said that, when he departed, Churchill first uttered the immortal words, "Never in the field of human conflict was so much owed by so many to so few," to Major-General Hastings Ismay, who had accompanied the PM on his visit. These words, of course, formed part of his famous speech made in the House of Commons a few days later. Churchill would be back at RAF Uxbridge on 15 September, when he famously asked Air Vice Marshall Sir Keith Park how many reserves he had, during what would turn out to be one of the most difficult days of the air battle. Park simply turned to the prime minister and told him, "There are none."

RAF Uxbridge, like so many other stations, was subjected to a number of air attacks during the Battle of Britain. Several such incidents occurred in September 1940 when, on the 26th, a delayed-action bomb hit the ground between the quarters of the WAAF and the police school, which had to be defused the following day. Several days later, on the 28th, another bomb lodged itself in a tree a mere 50 yards from the new operations room, which likewise had to be defused. Just over a week later, on 6 October, RAF Uxbridge was targeted by a Junkers 88, which dropped its ordnance on the local NAAFI which, although thankfully killed no-one, did cause disruption to the local gas and water supply.

Following the Battle of Britain, a Royal Box was installed in the operations room which, on 1 November 1940, was put to good use when King George VI and Queen Elizabeth visited in order for them to observe the work carried out in the nerve centre of No. 11 Group. Interestingly, a number

1. Hillingdon House, known as RAF Hillingdon, is today a Grade II listed building 2. A World War II air raid siren, removed from the roof of Hillingdon House in 1992 (Harrison49) 3. The former Officers' Mess building at RAF Uxbridge (Harrison49) 4. Three members of the Women's Auxiliary Air Force check rations in the store room at the Royal Air Force depot at Uxbridge 5. Trainees camping in 1938 before being posted to other units around the country 6. Women of the Women's Auxiliary Air Force catering section serve the lunchtime meal of steak and potatoes to queues of hungry airmen in 1944 7. The operations room at RAF Uxbridge, used by No. 11 Group of Fighter Command

of subsequently famous actors likewise visited the operations room later in the war; these included the likes of Rex Harrison (who was a Squadron Leader in the RAF at the time), Cyril Raymond (then an RAF fighter controller) and Ronald Adam (also a fighter controller).

As the war progressed, RAF Uxbridge saw a number of other units move in and changes take place. In 1941, a unit of the Meteorological Office was installed at the station, while a new RAF Station Hospital was formed from the WAAF hospital and the local sick quarters. The station also provided help in air support for the now infamous Operation Jubilee (the Dieppe Raid) on 19 August 1942, where Air Marshall Trafford Leigh-Mallory was placed in command of air forces supporting the operation, working from the operations room. Several years later, on 6 June 1944, RAF Uxbridge likewise saw the air forces of Operation

Overlord (D-Day) marshalled from the station's control room. Thus, RAF Uxbridge played both an important and prominent role during World War II.

After the war

Following the end of the war, RAF Uxbridge was used as the male athlete's village for the Summer Olympics of 1948, and the following year the RAF Cricket Association took up residence in Vine Lane, which was near to the station. Another unit to establish itself at RAF Uxbridge at this time was 14F Squadron of the Air Training Corps, a unit that still exists today, albeit at RAF Northolt.

In 1957, a granite memorial was installed above the operations rooms to recognise the men and women of No. 11 Group and their contribution to the war effort. It would be unveiled the following year by former Air Chief Marshal Hugh Dowding, and Douglas Bader also attended the ceremony. However,

at about this time, No. 11 Group departed RAF Uxbridge and moved to RAF Martlesham Heath. Interestingly, the operations room was then sealed off and left untouched in its original state. Hillingdon House passed to the Technical Training Command, and the RAF School of Education moved into the premises. RAF Uxbridge was then merged with No. 22 (Training) Group, and RAF Hillingdon and RAF Uxbridge would likewise be merged, the entirety now being known by the latter name.

RAF Uxbridge was granted the Freedom of the London Borough of Hillingdon in 1960, from which the personnel of the station gained the right to march through the borough in uniform. Later that year, the Queen's Colour Squadron of the RAF Regiment was stationed at RAF Uxbridge, and

the Southern Region Air Traffic Services was given new headquarters in Hillingdon House. While preparing for the shooting of the film the Battle of Britain, the preserved operations room at RAF Uxbridge was carefully examined in order to build a replica for the movie in 1968.

In early 1981, RAF Uxbridge was to become the target of the Irish Republican Army (IRA), who planted an explosive device in a barrack block. Fortunately, the device was discovered and the personnel of the barracks were removed to safety before it exploded. The following year, many of the men at the station were deployed in support of the Falklands War against Argentina, and in 1991 the station also deployed personnel to the Gulf during Operation *Granby* (Gulf War). In 2003, RAF Uxbridge again

supported operations in the Gulf, this time during Operation *Telic* (Iraq War).

By 2008, however, RAF Uxbridge was earmarked for closure, and became a satellite station of RAF Northolt. During its final years of operation, the station was home to the UK Airprox Board of the Civil Aviation Authority, which was based in Hillingdon House, and the Queen's Colour Squadron was given permission to parade through the centre of the town of Uxbridge following its return from a tour in Afghanistan in 2009. On 31 March 2010, RAF Uxbridge officially closed for good.

Today, those interested can visit the former operations room of No. 11 Group, which is now known as the Battle of Britain Bunker. It has been preserved to depict what the room looked like on 15 September 1940, the day of Winston Churchill's famous visit, at the height of the Battle of Britain.

Hillingdon House itself is now a Grade II listed building, and a number of the station's other original buildings still exist. As the visitor approaches the bunker, a replica Supermarine Spitfire can be seen outside, guarding the gate.

RAF MANSTON

A fighter base in two World Wars and a bastion of defence in the Cold War, Manston can claim to be one of the RAF's greatest front-line airfields

1

2

With World War I only 18 months into the slaughter across the Channel, the Admiralty decided to establish a military flying field just inland from the seaside town of Ramsgate in Kent. Ideally placed to defend the capital, Manston became a cornerstone for aerial operations in defence of the UK. The first huts were erected on the requisitioned farmland in February 1916 and aircraft began flying in May when a War Flight was set up. This was followed in September by a Handley Page Training Flight for crews to fly the large bombers.

In 1917, Manston began its defensive operations when, following ineffective Zeppelin raids over Britain the previous

RAF Manston

YEAR OPENED: 1916
YEAR CLOSED: 1999
SQUADRONS (WWII): No. 3 Squadron with Hurricanes, under the command of No. 11 Group Fighter Command. Then, 235, 253, 79 and 600. Followed by 54, 74, 4, 616 and 313
COMMANDER, 11 GROUP: Air Marshall Trafford Leigh-Mallory

year, the Germans began flying daylight attacks using large Gotha biplane bombers, firstly against Dover and Folkestone in May and subsequently against London. The Royal Flying Corps and Royal Naval Air Service responded by mounting interceptions of the heavily-defended enemy

political situation in Europe deteriorated.

The maelstrom of WWII

The new UK air defences, masterminded by RAF Fighter Command's Air Chief Marshal Sir Hugh Dowding, found Manston part of 11 Group under the command of the main Sector Station of Hornchurch (Sector D), along with Hawkinge, Gravesend and Rochford (now Southend). With war declared, a detachment of Hawker Hurricanes from No. 3 Sqn was assigned to the station from Croydon on September 10, 1939, in addition to No. 235 and 253 Sqns which reformed on the Fairey Battle light bomber. All were replaced by the end of the year with Hurricane-equipped 79 Sqn in October and 600 'City of London' Royal Auxiliary Air Force Sqn flying short-nose Blenheim IF fighters.

As operations gathered pace into 1940, one notable action involving Manston followed a report received in London on 10 May that German troops had begun invading Holland and requested a strike against the key airfield at Waalhaven near Rotterdam, in support of Dutch forces. The British Government ordered an attack, but not using bombers to avoid Dutch casualties, so six Manston-based Blenheim fighters from 'B' Flight 600 Sqn were dispatched. Led at low-level by Squadron Leader Jimmy Wells, five were lost intercepting Messerschmitt Bf 110s on the first pass over the target, while the sixth aircraft, piloted by Pilot Officer Norman Hayes destroyed a Ju 52 troop carrier on the ground, damaged a second which was preparing to land and attacked three Heinkel He111 bombers on his way back across the Channel. Hit and leaking fuel, Hayes managed to coax his badly damaged Blenheim back to Manston. He was subsequently awarded the DFC and his gunner received the DFM.

Later that month, Manston became pivotal in the RAF attempt to prevent or reduce attacks by the Luftwaffe on the troops of the British Expeditionary Force and units of the French army awaiting evacuation from the beaches of Dunkirk.

1. The old control tower at RAF Manston as it is today **2.** Wing Commander Roland Beamont when flying with 122 Wing, 2nd Tactical Air Force, just before being shot down in October 1944 and becoming a prisoner war **3.** Summer 1940 and a gunner prepares to man the four-gun turret of a Defiant fighter. Much was expected from the two-seater but the Luftwaffe quickly managed tactics to deal with it **4.** After the ravages wrought by the enemy in 1940, Manston was repaying the damage with new aircraft such as the Hawker Typhoon which operated in the fighter-bomber role from November 1942 **5.** Pictured in 1958, Manston's broad 3000-yard long runway with its adjacent crash bays remains one of the longest in Britain. At lower left, the large loop was used post-war by No.54 Maintenance Unit for dismantling aircraft

aircraft, but initially gained few successes. Manston-based fighters attacked the raiders again on 7 July and on 22 August brought down one of the aircraft near Vincent's Farm, close to the airfield.

Recognising Manston held a strong strategic position in the defence of London, the Admiralty ordered an expansion of the base with the construction of permanent hangars, workshops and accommodation for over 3,600 officers and men. Underground shelters were also constructed. The amalgamation of the RFC and RNAS into the Royal Air Force on April 1, 1918, resulted in the order for three bomber training squadrons to be established at Manston with the War Flight expanded to three

flights to form 219 Squadron. After the Armistice in November 1918, the airfield became a demobilisation centre for the thousands of men and women returning from France and in 1920 the first elements of the School of Technical Training (Men) moved in.

Despite post-war cut-backs, married quarters were built in the mid-1920s. This period also saw expansion and improved facilities as Manston was camouflaged and given storage for up to 40t of bombs and five million rounds of small arms ammunition. Newly-dug trenches, blast shelters for aircraft and personnel, and improved anti-aircraft defences also appeared – elements that would prove vital as the

Fighter squadrons of 11 Group charged with patrols in the vicinity of the Belgian port forward-operated from Manston during daylight hours before returning to their home bases at the end of each day. Contrary to the impression given by the hard-pressed troops on the beaches, the RAF was heavily engaged trying to keep the enemy from bombing the British forces and this required combat out of eyeshot of the soldiers. Between 26 May and 3 June of Operation *Dynamo*, the Dunkirk evacuation, more than 70 RAF pilots were lost or taken prisoner, many of them flying from Manston.

May also saw the first bombing attacks on the Kent airfield, but damage was light and in response No.1 'M' Balloon unit arrived to add more protection to the base. June was a relatively quiet month as the Germans settled into their new airfields along the French and Belgian coast, but on 3 July a handful of Do 17s suddenly appeared, scattering light bombs across the airfield which produced no material damage. Fighter Command's defensive commander, Air Marshal Sir Keith Park ordered various squadrons to forward deploy to Manston through the following weeks with No.s 54, 74 and 41 Sqn all taking turns to counter the skirmishing by the Luftwaffe as the attacks began to chip away at the RAF's defensive airfields.

However, on 12 August the Luftwaffe returned in force when 15 Bf 110s and some He111s swept in to bomb from low altitude damaging two hangars, destroying workshops and killing one civilian. More attacks followed with low-level bombing and machine gunning claiming aircraft destroyed on the ground on 14 August, including three Blenheim fighters and four hangars destroyed. The following day, 15 August, a snap raid by 12 Bf 110s sprayed the base with bombs and cannon fire inflicting 16 casualties and destroying two Spitfires.

Through these and later operations, Manston had become a target of opportunity for the Luftwaffe as aircraft returned to their continental bases and damage became widespread with personnel constantly aware that they were very much in the front-line of the Battle. As administrative buildings and offices were destroyed, it was decided that all non-essential personnel should be accommodated off site at Westgate. To raise the spirits of the hard-pressed defenders, Prime Minister Winston Churchill visited the airfield on 28 August and inspected the extensive damage. Coincidentally, Churchill's visit was the day the RAF withdrew the turreted Boulton-Paul Defiant fighter from daylight operations, the type having suffered high losses in combat with the Germans. The PM subsequently wrote to the Secretary of State and Chief of Air Staff that he was perturbed it was taking so much time to repair the aerodromes, suggesting mobile

1. Manston was host to Westland Whirlwinds in spring 1943 when No. 137 Sqn was busily engaged in bombing attacks on shipping and near-continental targets. Crews take a break with the CO, Sqn Ldr Coghlan (third from right) **2.** An Air Ministry map issued in September 1945 giving location and runway details for RAF Manston. Airfield control used the call sign 'Bluefrock'

repair companies should be established.

With the enemy frustrated that the RAF continued to engage them in considerable numbers through September and into October, the Luftwaffe switched to night-bombing London while the single-seat fighters were fitted with belly-mounted bombs and developed fast, hit-and-run, daylight attacks against airfields, radar stations and towns. In the ruins of Manston, new arrivals were the Westland Lysanders of No 4 Army Co-operation Sqn which were assigned to assist in the rescue of downed aircrew around the immediate sea areas, in co-operation with the high speed rescue launches operating out of Ramsgate harbour.

Through 1941 and into 1942, Manston doubled its role with anti-shipping strikes by Fairey Albacores of the Fleet Air Arm against enemy vessels adding to its 11 Group task of operating fighters. However, emerging was a new duty, that of a haven for crippled aircraft returning from continental missions, typified by the night of 28-29 August 1942, when 11 damaged or short of fuel bombers made landfall at the Kent base.

The oft-repeated request for a suitable runway for this unique role finally bore fruit when, on 15 June 1943, builders John Laing & Son began work to meet a contract for a

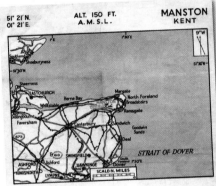
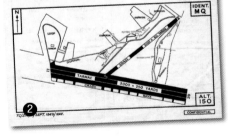

3,000yd tarmac runway, 250yd wide with crash bays, roads, lighting and drainage. While under construction, the airfield remained operational and on 5 April 1944, the new runway was finished. Within three weeks, 56 emergency landings were recorded! British and American aircrew were briefed on the new emergency runway and Manston joined Woodbridge in Suffolk and Carnaby in Yorkshire in offering this facility.

By June, more than 700 aircraft had touched down on Manston's welcoming runway and a special casualty centre was set up for those needing urgent medical attention. An additional aid was the installation of FIDO – Fog Investigation and Dispersal Operation – whereby petrol burners were

1. In August 1944, Hawker Tempest's of No. 501 'County of Gloucester' Sqn arrived at Manston to assist with anti-'Diver' patrols to combat the German V1 flying-bomb campaign against London 2. The final RAF involvement in Manston was the operation of SAR helicopters with No. 22 Sqn Wessex in use until withdrawal in July 1994 3. When operating as an emergency landing airfield, one of the larger RAF aircraft to use the facility was Vickers Valiant WZ396 of No. 543 Sqn on May 23, 1964 4. The US Eighth Air Force arrived in 1943 5. One of the last users of the Spitfire at the airfield was No.313 Czechoslovak Sqn equipped with Mk IXs. Arriving in February 1945, the squadron undertook a number of 'Ramrod' sweeps over Europe

installed along the runway to disperse fog and in one month in September 1944, FIDO assisted in the safe return of 19 bombers.

On July 21, 1944, two of Britain's latest jet fighters, Gloster Meteor F.1s, arrived as the urgent vanguard of others to equip 616 Sqn, their role being the fast interception of unmanned V1 flying bombs being launched against London. The squadron diarist wrote: 'The Meteors go into operation. History is made!' The first Diver patrol, as these sorties against the V1 were called, was flown by Flying Officer McKenzie who took off from Manston at 2.30pm on 27 July, but with no success. Gun jamming was an early problem with the new jets and it was Flight Officer 'Dixie' Dean who solved this difficulty when he met up with one of the deadly winged bombs on 4 August. When the guns duly jammed, he flew the Meteor alongside the V1 for nearly half a minute gradually manoeuvring his wing tip under the wing of the bomb before pulling upwards and tipping it over on its back sending it to earth some four miles south of Tonbridge. By the time the launch sites were overrun, 616 Sqn had destroyed 13 V1s.

In August, the US Eighth Air Force posted a special 250-strong detachment to the base, the 16th Mobile Reclamation and Repair Squadron to handle the large number of damaged B-17s and B-24 bombers, plus P-47 Thunderbolts and P-51 Mustang fighters, that were arriving from the massed bombing operations over Europe. Some were short of fuel, but most made landfall with various amounts of damage from German Flak and fighters.

With the end of the European war, Manston became a staging post for Transport Command with civil operator Skyways flying Avro Yorks to the Middle East. Operations changed again on 14 July 1950, when the airfield came under the control of RAF Fighter Command to allow rotational visits by military jets of the United States Air Force. Later that month, 70 Republic F-84 Thunderjets of the 20th Fighter-Bomber Wing swept into the Kent base to begin

nearly a decade of rotational operations in support of the US Third Air Force bombers flying from more northerly airfields in the UK. So began the airfield's Cold War phase. The straight-wing Thunderjets were replaced in turn by swept-wing F-86F Sabres and the all-weather North American F-86D Sabre 'Dogs' of the 406th Fighter-Bomber Wing before these visits ended in May 1958. To support the atomic-bomb carrying jets, a squadron of Grumman SA-16 Albatross amphibians took up residence to haul pilots out of the cold English Channel when the temperamental jet engines stopped working!

While the airfield retained its emergency landing status, it closed briefly before returning to No.11 Group Fighter Command linked to RAF West Malling. Search and rescue helicopters, initially Whirlwinds of No. 22 SAR Sqn operated from the base, followed by a three-year period when civilian contractor Bristow Helicopters took on the role. The RAF resumed the task with a Wessex Flight from 1975 and this continued until July 1994 when the ASR role moved to RAF Wattisham. Manston finally closed as a flying base on March 31, 1999. Plans remain to return the airfield to flying status for air freight operations – but the demand for housing in southeast Kent remains strong.

RAF BRIZE NORTON

The largest RAF station, home to strategic and tactical air transport and air-to-air refuelling

Royal Air Force Brize Norton was officially opened on 13 August 1937, following several years of construction that had begun in 1935. It is normal for RAF stations to be named after the nearest town or village, but since the station was predominately within the parish of Carterton in Oxfordshire, there was concern that there might be some confusion with RAF Cardington in Bedfordshire. As such, it was decided to name it RAF Brize Norton, which was the next-nearest town to the new station. The following month after its opening, No. 2 Flying Training School became the first unit to be based at Brize Norton after it transferred from RAF Digby, although building work at the station had in fact not

RAF Brize Norton

YEAR OPENED: 1937
YEAR CLOSED: Still open
CURRENT SQUADRONS: 10, 24, 30, 47, 70, 99, 101
STATION COMMANDER: Group Captain Timothy T Jones BSc(Hons) MA RAF

yet been completed. Just over a year later No. 6 Maintenance Unit also arrived. The main purpose of the station was for flying training, although a detachment of No. 110 Squadron from RAF Wattisham operated Bristol Blenheims MK Is and Mk IVs from Brize Norton in 1939. In July 1942 it became home to the Heavy Glider Conversion Unit (HGCU), which remained at the

1. Brize Norton was tasked with supplying emergency relief to the British Virgin Islands after the devastation of Hurricane Irma (RAF/MoD) **2.** In addition to flying training, Brize Norton became home to the Heavy Glider Conversion Unit **3.** North American Harvards of No. 2 Flying Training School, based at Brize Norton **4.** A C17 of No. 99 Squadron taking off from Brize Norton in 2013 (Paul Crouch/MoD) **5.** Aerial photographs showing the development of Brize Norton in 1957, 1965, 1975 and 1989 respectively

station until December 1945.

On 16 August 1940, Brize Norton was attacked by German bombers, which saw the destruction of 35 Airspeed Oxfords and 11 Hawker Hurricanes. In 1942, the detachment of No. 110 Squadron left for service in the Far East. Later, between March and October 1944, Brize Norton was used for parachute and glider opera-

tions by Nos. 296 and 297 Squadrons, both of which operated Armstrong Whitworth Albemarle twin-engine transport aircraft. These two squadrons would, on D-Day, be employed in dropping paratroopers and towing Horsa Gliders, which were given the task of capturing bridges located six miles inland over the River Orne and Caen Canal. The squadrons also launched two

other gliders in order to capture a coastal battery that commanded the estuary of the River Orne. Following these successful operations, the same Brize Norton based squadrons supported Operation Market Garden, landing troops near Arnhem in September 1944.

Following the end of WWII, Brize Norton became home to the Transport Com-

1. One of the North American Harvards of No. 2 Flying Training School, based at Brize Norton 2. A Vickers VC10 K2 of No. 101 Squadron at Brize Norton in 1985 (Mike Freer) 3. An Atlas A400M coming in to land at Brize Norton in 2014 (MoD/Crown Copyright) 4. A C-130J Hercules of No. 47 Squadron taxing at Brize Norton in 2016 (Paul Crouch) 5. Aid being loaded onto a Hercules at Brize Norton for air drop over northern Iraq (Steve Lympany/MOD)

mand Development Unit and the School of Flight Efficiency. The following year, the Army Airborne Transport Development Unit also moved in. For a brief period between August 1949 and June 1950, the station once again returned to the business of flying training, with No. 204 Advanced Flying Training School, equipped with De Havilland Mosquitoes, taking up residence. However, on 16 April 1951, Brize Norton was officially placed under the control of the United States Air Force, which almost immediately set about developing the station for its own needs, including extending the runway and building a number of new accommodation blocks.

The first American aircraft to be briefly stationed at Brize Norton were 21 B-36 Convair 'Peacemaker' strategic bombers of the 11th Bombardment Wing, which arrived in June 1952. These were followed by the B-29 Superfortresses of the 301st Bombardment Wing in December. The following year, a number of B-47E Stratojet long-range strategic bombers arrived and, in December 1954, these were joined by a number of Boeing KC-97G Stratofreighters.

Brize Norton remained the home of a number of USAF bomber wings and refuelling squadrons until April 1965.

As the USAF departed Brize Norton, the RAF moved back in, it again becoming a base for Transport Command and the subsequent Air Support Command from 1967. The station continued to expand in numbers of personnel during this period, as it became the Strategic Air Transport base for the RAF. A new £2 million Base Hangar was also built, which at the time was the largest cantilever structure in western Europe, as well as the Gateway House hotel. Brize Norton also became home to No. 99 and 511 Squadrons, which operated Bristol Britannia aircraft, and No. 10 Squadron, which was equipped with Vickers VC10s. Later, in June 1970, these units were joined by No. 53 Squadron, which flew Short Belfast heavy lift aircraft. By 1972, Brize Norton was part of No. 46 Group of RAF Strike Command,

before transferring to No. 38 Group in 1975.

In the mid-1970s, No. 53, 99 and 511 Squadrons fell victim to the Defence White Paper of 1974, and all were disbanded. No. 10 Squadron, however, continued to operate from Brize Norton, which was joined by No. 115 Squadron in 1976. This latter unit was equipped with Armstrong Whitworth Argosy aircraft, although these were replaced later by Hawker Siddeley Andovers. Also in 1976, the Joint Air Transport Establishment, No. 38 Group Tactical Communications Wing (TCW) and No. 1 Parachute Training School moved into the station. No. 115 Squadron, however, moved out to RAF Benson in 1982.

During the Falklands conflict, many in the TCW were sent to the Ascension Island, with No. 10 Squadron transporting personnel and supplies to the island from the UK. The squadron was also involved in the transportation of wounded and following the end of the conflict carried out a re-supply function for the newly established Falklands garrison.

Brize Norton also played a major supporting role during the Gulf War of 1990-91, when No. 101 Squadron and elements of No. 216 Squadron were sent to the Gulf. Both squadrons performed an air-

to-air refuelling (AAR) function, providing support not only to RAF combat aircraft in the region but also to those of the US Navy and US Marine Corps. Many of the TCW personnel also deployed to the Gulf direct from Brize Norton.

By the early 1990s, Brize Norton had become the hub for all AAR operations for the RAF. The station was also host to a number of large tanker deployments from the USAF, including those which supported air operations during the Kosovo campaign of 1999. In addition to the USAF, the tankers of the RAF, including aircraft from No. 10, 101 and 216 Squadrons, took an active role.

⑤

The station passed to No. 2 Group in April 2000, with No. 99 Squadron and its Boeing C-17 Globemaster III strategic transport aircraft arriving to take up a new home. Brize Norton subsequently supported operations in both Afghanistan and Iraq, with seven aircraft and 500 personnel deploying in support of the former and 12 aircraft and 600 personnel to the latter.

When RAF Lyneham closed in late 2011, the repatriation of British personnel was conducted through Brize Norton from 8 September. In order to facilitate this, a new purpose-built centre was erected, while an exit gate was fully refurbished and renamed 'Britannia Gate'. Further refurbishment of some 70 buildings was completed by the middle of the same year as part of a large project to improve the infrastructure.

RAF Brize Norton remains an active and busy station for the RAF, serving as home for the entire AAR and Strategic Air Transport fleets, and is the largest RAF station in the UK. Current squadrons include: No. 10 (Voyager KC2/KC3); No. 24 (Hercules C4/C5 and A400M Atlas); No. 30 (Hercules C4/C5); No. 47 (Hercules (C4/C5); No. 70 (A400M Atlas); No. 99 (C-17 Globemaster III); and No. 101 (Voyager KC2/KC3).

The personnel at the station are ready, 24 hours a day, to support operations or respond to crises worldwide. Recently, a state of emergency was declared by the British Virgin Islands after Hurrican Irma. RAF Brize Norton was asked to deliver aid and personnel to help with the recovery of devastated areas. In the first week alone, some 376,529kg of freight left the station to provide disaster relief.

THE RAF STRATEGY: A FORCE FOR THE FUTURE

How a new RAF strategy will meet the UK defence and security needs

Words Chris Duffill

1. A Tornado GR4 at RAF Marham (SAC Andy Masson/MOD) 2. No.1 Squadron RAF Regiment on Parade (Sgt Ralph Merry ABIPP RAF/MOD) 3. A Young RAF Recruit Smiles on Parade at RAF Halton (Kate Parrott/MOD) 4. A Royal Air Force Tornado GR4 pilot with IX (Bomber) Squadron (Sgt Paul Oldfield/MOD) 5. RAF Tornados Leaving Afghanistan (Corporal Andrew Morris (RAF)/MOD)

The RAF has a proud history that stretches back a hundred years. During that time it has filled a multi-faceted role in both war and peacetime, from defending our skies to international operations and extending the UKs power and influence.

In recent years the Force's reach and capabilities have been tested and proven in various high-profile operations, from the Gulf War in 1991 to Kosovo in 1999 and recent conflicts in Iraq and Afghanistan. Active operations have included high-intensity fighting, humanitarian missions, transport logistics, the policing of no-fly zones, and supporting the UN in several capacities from the Balkans to Africa.

Given the ongoing importance of overseas and domestic operations, the RAF is at the forefront of the Government's periodic Strategic Defence and Security Review. The 2015 review announced that the MOD would be spending an extra twelve billion pounds on the RAF, raising its ten-year equipment budget to £178 billion. This increase has been seen as an opportunity for evolution as well as growth.

Today the RAF is comprised of around 39,400 uniformed staff. Together they operate from twelve bases within the UK and also a number of overseas airfields, operating 1,100 aircraft. To deliver its ongoing mission the organisation employs four main capabilities: Air Control, Mobility, Intelligence, and Attack. These work collectively to win and maintain air-superiority that is fundamental to any theatre of operations, and these variable needs are reflected in the diversity of current RAF aircraft and technology.

Current attack platforms include the Tornado GR.4 and Eurofighter Typhoon, the former being the RAFs primary offensive platform with over 30 years of service and currently present in Kandar, Afghanistan. Their enhanced weaponry comprises a formidable array of firepower – with DMS Brimstone and Paveway IV Precision Guided Munitions, a 27mm gun and the Litening III air-to-ground targeting system.

The RAFs mobility role to deliver aid, strategic transports and tactical-airlifts is carried out by the four-engine Hercules C-130K capable of carrying up to 128 passengers or 20 tonnes of freight, and the Airbus A400M Atlas. These are joined by the Boeing C-17 Globemaster II in a heavy strategic airlift role, and the Airbus A330 MRTT for more routine transport tasks. The Voyager performs air-to-air refuelling.

RAF helicopters, such as the Puma HC2 and the twin-rotor Chinook, support the British Army ground units and Royal Marines with firepower and heavy-lift capabilities. Air Transport and Search and Rescue tasks are carried out by the Griffin

1

HAR2, and the A-109 Power Elite.

In order to act with efficiency and precision, all of these capabilities are underpinned by the RAFs intelligence role (Information, Surveillance, Target Acquisition, and Reconnaissance). Early warning systems such as the Sentry AEW1 at RAF Waddington are joined by the Sentinel R1 and Beechcraft Shadow R1 jet-aircraft mounted ground radar surveillance systems to detect incoming enemy aircraft and coordinate the battlefield. Satellite imagery works in tandem with weapon-aiming sensors on combat jets such as the Tornado and Typhoon to perform target acquisition, further aided by cameras and infra-red sensors. MQ-9 Reaper unmanned

aerial vehicles support operations in Afghanistan and Iraq through high-altitude surveillance, armed with laser-guided bombs and air-to-ground missiles.

However impressive its capabilities and achievements, the nature of warfare, security and defence is continually evolving and the RAF must periodically reassess its needs and review its strategy. With an increased MOD budget to underpin it, there is now a renewed emphasis on technology and intelligence under a highly skilled and professional workforce.

This new approach will shape and guide the RAFs growth up to the year 2025, forming a fully modernised strategy for an increasingly complex world.

1. RAF Chinook creates a huge dust cloud during a resupply to 42 Commando in Afghanistan (Sean Clee/MOD) 2. An RAF F-35B Lightning II flying over RAF Marham, Norfolk (Cpl Paul Oldfield/MOD) 3. Tornado GR.4 training for deployment to Afghanistan (Corporal Mike Jones/MOD) 4. RAF Eurofighter Typhoon based at RAF Coningsby firing an ASRAAM missile (Geoffrey Lee/MOD)

A sizeable share of the RAF's budget is, of course, still spent on aircraft. The MOD recently received its first Lightning II Joint Strike Fighter – the Lockheed Martin F-35B, a single-seat, single-engine stealth fighter designed for ground attack and air superiority missions. It is due to enter service in 2018. Two further Eurofighter squadrons are also planned, and Apache attack and Chinook support helicopters will also see upgrades. Pilot training aircraft are due to be replaced with new models such as the Embraer Phenom 100.

In the intelligence sphere, there are three additional Beechcraft Shadow R1 aircraft. Three more Boeing RC-135W Rivet Joint reconnaissance jets were also introduced for the interception and decoding of communications, alongside a fleet of P-8 Maritime Patrol Aircraft that provide overland surveillance as well as aerial anti-submarine capability. The replacement of the Reaper UAV fleet with a fleet of Protector remotely-piloted armed surveillance aircraft with enhanced range is also underway.

Technology aside, the RAF prides itself on the quality and professionalism of its people. The extended budget granted to it by the Strategic Review further enables a recruitment drive to find, train and develop a skilled workforce across a wide range of roles and disciplines. The RAF recruitment programme offers roles such as aircrew (pilots, weapons operators), air traffic control and flight operations managers; logistics, medical, intelligence, and engineering. There are currently 22 RAF apprenticeship courses available.

With expansion well under-way, the Royal Air Force is meeting the defence, warfare and security challenges of the 21st Century. Future conflicts with agile and technically capable adversaries require a new full-spectrum response; from tackling ambiguous 'hybrid' warfare and cyber-aided offensives to fighting traditional war and undertaking peacetime operations. Through the focused investment in both technology and people, the new RAF strategy is creating a next generation Air Force.

CAREERS IN THE RAF

Being a pilot isn't the only way to become a high-flyer

Words Chris Duffill

Today's RAF is a powerhouse of national recruitment, providing thousands of jobs across a wide array of skills and professions. The organisation has evolved from its roots as a somewhat temporary organisation designed to fight World War I to a keystone of the UKs military establishment. Back in 1919, Churchill appointed Major-General Hugh Trenchard as Chief of The Air Staff to put together a 'Scheme for the Permanent Organization of the Royal Air Force'. Trenchard's vision was to place training at the heart of the service. His emphasis on providing airmen and officers with highly specialised skills laid the foundation for the RAFs approach to training and recruitment. This has led to a lasting commitment to provide solid career opportunities for both school-leavers and older people looking for a career change.

Many assume that a career in the RAF means aerial combat and pilot training, and for some this is gladly the case, but the modern air force is a fully inclusive organisation with a wide-spectrum role – from delivering humanitarian aid and preventing war, to providing transport logistics, intelligence services, cyberspace communications, and even hosting ceremonial events. Despite the clear occupational hazards involved in being a pilot, aircrew, or other personnel deployed into war zones, the RAF is known as the safest of the three main branches of the armed forces.

Behind every front-line operation and airbase there are thousands of people who underpin the organisation, including engineers, pilots, and firefighters; but also photographers, caterers and musicians. With over 50 diverse opportunities currently on offer, if a job exists in the civilian world the chances are that the RAF will have a similar role available.

Careers in the RAF are broadly divided into two categories: Regulars, and Reserves. RAF Regulars are full-time personnel who serve in the UK, and possibly abroad, as a crucial part of our defence and peacekeeping operations. RAF Reserves train for and perform their role in their spare time, often working around their day-job. They work alongside Regulars to gain transferable

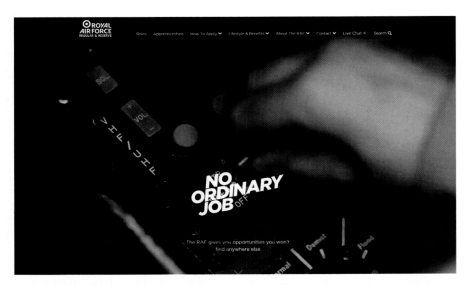

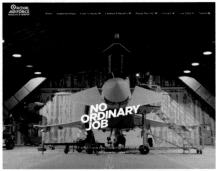

The current advertising for the RAF emphasis the variety of roles available

skills and experience that can often apply to their career outside the service. Both paths provide exciting work and a rewarding lifestyle with opportunities for advancement.

Regardless of whether someone is a Regular or a Reserve, the RAF, like most large organisations, relies on a strong internal management structure. Each role is accompanied by a rank which defines the level of responsibility. There are three rank structures: Commissioned Officers, Airmen and Airwomen, and, finally, non-Commissioned Aircrew.

Officers perform the RAFs management role and as such they command and lead others. The lowest officer rank is Pilot Officer, ascending via Squadron Leader,

Group Captain and others all the way to Air Chief Marshal. Officer training is distinct from other areas of RAF training due to the command and management aspect of the rank. All Pilots must also undergo officer training and many ground support roles such as Engineer require officers to manage their teams. Royal Air Force College Cranwell in Lincolnshire is home to the RAF's training and education academy for officer cadets – another facet of Trenchard's legacy as the 'Father of The RAF'. Flight training is carried out at various facilities around the UK.

Airmen and Airwomen form the majority of RAF personnel and play a vital role in ground support and other specialist areas. Although they don't enter as officers, they

A Royal Air Force Firefighter tackles flames at the Defence Fire Training and Development Centre, Manston (Crown Copyright)

1. Trainee RAF pilots on a training flight in Grob Light Aircraft (RAF/MoD) 2. The crew of a RAF Griffin helicopter of the Defence Helicopter Flying School practices approaches to the runway (Ian Forshaw, Crown Copyright) 3. A Royal Air Force Police Dog Handler releases his Air Dog (MoD/Crown Copyright) 4. A Royal Air Force Station Warrant Officer salutes at a Parade at RAF Cosford (Cpl Hammond, MoD/Crown Copyright) 5. A pilot from 39 Sqn remotely controls a Reaper MQ-9 UAV during a training sortie (SAC Andrew Morris, Crown Copyright) 6. The Officer's Mess at Royal Air Force College Cranwell

can apply for a commission later in their career as they gain skills and experience. Examples of rank in this category include Senior Aircraftman/Aicraftwoman, Lance Corporal, and Chief Technician. The Warrant Officer is at the top of this structure. Roles include everything from technical and engineering (Electricians, Cyberspace Communication Specialists, Aircraft Technicians) to support roles such as Air Cartographer and Flight Operations Assistant; plus RAF Police, Drivers,

Nurses, Physical Training Instructors and Intelligence Analysts.

Non-Commissioned Aircrew occupy a special category as they undertake flight missions in roles such as weapons systems operators, aircrew responsible for payload, or acoustics operators working on reconnaissance aircraft. They don't need to become Officers (as RAF Pilots have to) even though they hold distinctive highly-operational positions.

There are currently 22 apprenticeship

roles to choose from and the RAF provides pay during training. Apprentices can expect a civilian qualification and a guaranteed job at the end of their course. More experienced candidates may not require an RAF apprenticeship, as they will apply directly for a job using their existing skills and qualifications, but there is always an element of training for new recruits.

Unlike further education for civilians, training cannot be provided by the usual assortment of colleges or universities.

Going back to 1919, and Trenchard's vision for an RAF with training at its core, he maintained that the organisation should train its own people as that would pass on the Air Force spirit to its recruits. As a result apprenticeships are taught at main training bases such as Cranwell and RAF Halton in Buckinghamshire. However, in October 2016 the RAF launched the UK's first Air & Defence Career College in collaboration with Lincoln College. It specialises in engineering, computer science, and catering. Once a

course is completed 16-18 year-olds are guaranteed a place on the RAF Basic Recruit Training course afterwards.

RAF recruits live in on-base accommodation during initial training – ten weeks for Airmen/Airwomen and 24 weeks for Officers. Due to the nature of the work, in many cases there are age, health and qualification requirements; up to date information on careers and apprenticeships can be found on the RAF's website at **www. raf.mod.uk/recruitment**.

So, with an eclectic mix of careers on offer such as Survival Equipment Specialist, Chef, Biomedical Scientist and Photographer the RAF colleges are much more than just schools for pilots.

Today's school-leavers and graduates who embark on a career in the Royal Air Force will bring with them their talent and determination to succeed – a fitting reflection of the RAF motto of 'Per Ardua ad Astra', which is, of course, 'Through Adversity to the Stars'.

RAF MEMORIALS

Memorials, monuments and flights dedicated to the Royal Air Force and those who flew to defend our liberty

Words Garrett Eriksen

They found his body washed up on the start and stony shore of Trondheim, Norway. He was dressed in the uniform of Her Majesty's Royal Air Force, Scottish regiment, but also had South African Air Force insignia on the tattered remains of his uniform. They found no other identifiers on his person, apart from the name stitched on to the chest of his shirt: G. B. Callaghan, and the stripes on his shoulder signifying the rank of lieutenant. Despite this, his death would remain a mystery, not only for those who chose to honour him by burying him in the frozen ground of a melancholy Norwegian graveyard, but also for his family back in then Rhodesia (today Zimbabwe) for many years to come.

As the year was 1943 identification was impossible until, in the early '90s, a Norwegian civil engineer and his son decided to attempt to track down the family of the mysterious Lt. G. B. Callaghan, who had never been claimed and whose grave had never been visited except by the locals who had buried him. This is how my mother learnt of the fate of her missing grandfather. In many ways his grave is a war monument. It attests that he was alive and did his duty and flew magnificently. That monument is well known in our family, and is the subject of occasional pilgrimage and a place we can share our history with the younger members. Its importance cannot be understated, and this is just a simple grave and one family's story.

How important, then, are other war monuments that honour hundreds and thousands of men and women who paid the ultimate price fighting the most important war of the last hundred years? And, in the case of the RAF, where does one go to pay their respects to past aircrew? Their battles were in the sky and not tied down to specific locales as is the case with many other memorials. Many towns and cities will have memorials dedicated to several battles, events or people, but only a handful of RAF memorials exist in the UK. However, these memorials are often breath-taking and

The cemetery in Trondheim is the largest Commonwealth war grave plot in Norway

A 1940 poster honouring RAF achievements, featuring a quote from Prime Minister Churchill

do an excellent job at demonstrating the importance of the RAF during World War II and honouring their sacrifices. Here then is a list of some of the most well-known, and some upcoming, memorials and monuments dedicated to the RAF.

Battle of Britain memorials

The Battle of Britain is perhaps the most famous military campaign undertaken by the RAF. From 10 July to 31 October 1940 almost 2,000 British and Canadian aircraft defended the UK from Luftwaffe incursion, defending against a force of over 2,500 German aircraft. Though civilian and military casualties were heavy, the defence was successful and arguably enforced an already firm backbone of Allied resistance against Nazi forces. Since 1943, 15 September has been known as the Battle of Britain Day and often sees memorial parades and flights in honour of the RAF.

The Battle has several notable memorials around England, however three in particular stand out. The first is the monument located on the White Cliffs at Capel-le-Ferne, on

The Battle of Britain memorial at Capel-le-Ferne as soon from above

the coast of Kent which was commissioned by the Battle of Britain Memorial Trust and dedicated by Queen Elizabeth in July of 1993. The outdoor monument's paths form a large propeller-shape radiating outwards from a seated pilot in the centre who is staring out over the English Channel.

The site, opened in 2015, is notable for having a fascinating visitor centre built in the shape of a Spitfire wing. It features several multimedia interactive experiences and information centres to give visitors an in-depth understanding of RAF battles and especially of the Battle of Britain. The site also hosts replicas of two well-known aircraft: the Spitfire and the Hurricane. A more traditional, but no less impactful, memorial wall is also present and lists the names of 3,000 aircraft crew who were involved in the Battle of Britain. Find out more at: **www.battleofbritainmemorial.org/ visit/visit-the-memorial/welcome/**

A second, and more recent memorial, is the Battle of Britain Monument in London which was opened in 2005, on the 65th anniversary of the Battle, and is located at the Victoria Embankment, overlooking the Thames River. This monument was opened in the presence of several surviving RAF members, known colloquially as The Few after Winston Churchill's famous quote, "Never was so much owed by so many to

A relief of RAF pilots in action displayed on the Battle of Britain Monument in London

so few," wherein he honoured the ongoing efforts of the RAF.

The 25m-long monument commemorates pilots lost during the Battle, including those from other Allied countries. It is made of bronze and granite and has several stylised reliefs of pilots and aircrew scrambling for their aircraft to defend their homes, amongst other scenes. Learn more about it at: **www.bbm.org.uk**

A sculpture of a seated RAF pilot at Capel-le-Ferne, overlooking the English Channel

The third memorial is not a monument but rather an event, or, in their own words, a 'museum without walls'. The RAF Battle of Britain Memorial Flight was formed in 1957 and is group dedicated to a single mission: 'To maintain and fly historic RAF bombers and fighters, to provide members of the public with the sight and sound of a by gone age and to stay a living and breathing tribute to those who paid the ultimate sacrifice.'

A Lancaster Bomber, Spitfire and Hurricane make up the core of this aerial display with a further nine aircraft joining the flight depending on the event. The group also maintains a Visitor's Centre in Coningsby, Lincolnshire. Unlike more static monuments, the flights are used to instil a sense of tactile history in their audience and the visitor's centre allow for a guided tour of the aircraft when not in use. Support the flight here: **www.raf.mod.uk/bbmf/**

Bomber Command

High on the list of important memorials to visit would be the RAF Bomber Command Memorial in Green Park, London. Opened in June of 2012 the memorial commemorates over 55,000 aircrew and civilians from around the Commonwealth who either gave their lives in service of the RAF or who were killed in bombings and raids during WWII. The names of aircrew who survived are also included on the monument as well.

Controversy has often surrounded the tactics used by Bomber Command during WWII, notably the bombing of civilian centres, dams and other arguably 'non-military' targets. This controversy, combined with funding issues, delayed the construction of many RAF monuments and especially those dedicated to bombers, but a resurgence in support has seen a rise of such memorials in the last decade. Dam Busters enjoy something of a heroic status in the RAF community, along with dogfighters and ace pilots, and have been the subject of public attention recently with a spate of films and books on the subject. The raider crews have finally seen their efforts become commemorated in monument form and, to quote veteran pilot Alan Finch, it is, "bloody marvellous." Support Bomber Command's efforts here: **www.rafbf.org/bomber-command-memorial**

Runnymede Memorial

The Airforces Memorial in Englefield Green near Surrey, also called the Runnymede Memorial, is the largest memorial on this list and hosts the names of over 20,000 men and women, from multiple Commonwealth countries, who were involved in the RAF during WWII.

The specific purpose of this memorial is to list those with no known grave

1. The core group of the BBMF: Lancaster Bomber (centre), Supermarine Spitfire (bottom) and Hawker Hurricane (top) **2.** The Bomber Command Memorial in London, unveiled by Queen Elizabeth II in 2012 **3.** The entrance to the Runnymede Memorial in Englefield

in any part of the world. Thus, many commemorated here have never had their remains found or simply vanished in the line of duty and were never commemorated.

Built in 1953, the building hosts several wings with a variety of plaques, insignia and monuments dotted around the landscape all revealing the names of those lost. A restful setting befitting a memorial, the building overlooks the Thames River and the Runnymede Meadow. If your family is missing a loved one from this era, this might be a good place to start: **www.cwgc.org/find/find-cemeteries-and-memorials/109600/runnymede-memorial**

1. A gilded eagle atop an armillary sphere depicting the zodiac heads the RAF monument **2.** A variety of commemorative trees and monuments dot the landscape of this 150acre memorial **3.** A Lancaster Bomber does a fly past over the newly built IBCM spire

Royal Airforce Memorial

The oldest memorial on this list, the Royal Airforce Memorial was unveiled in 1923 and stands tall on the Victoria Embankment in London. Initially created to list the aircrew lost during the Great War, it was expanded in 1946 to include the names of those lost in World War II and is considered by and large to be the official memorial dedicated to the RAF and related services.

The monument is made from Portland stone and features a gilded eagle perched atop a globe preparing to take flight as well as several inscriptions on each face of the central pillar.

On 15 September every year, to commemorate Battle of Britain Day, and the RAF fallen, the Chief of Air Staff places a wreath at the foot of the monument in a solemn and impactful service. Two sides of the monument bear the motto of the RAF: Per ardua ad astra (Through adversity to the stars). Support the memorial fund here: www.rafbf.org/about-us/raf-memorial

National Memorial Arboretum

Arguably one of the most beautiful memorials on this list, the National Memorial Arboretum is a living memorial where trees have been planted in honour of those who lost their lives in service to,

not only the RAF, but the Armed Forces as a whole. Built in 2001, the monument is located at Alrewas, near Staffordshire, and boasts 150 acres of trees, memorials and monuments. 50,000 trees are planted there and more are added every year with the site also being a collection point for monuments and plaques that are no longer being cared for by previous owners or governing bodies, so that they might always have a final resting place.
Learn more at: www.thenma.org.uk

The Future of Memorials

January of 2018 will see a new International Bomber Command Centre opening at Canwick Hill in Lincoln. The centre is taking memorials a step further and is not only providing traditional memorial space in the forms of walls and monuments, but is combining interactive multimedia elements, a museum including artefacts, displays and archives, tours and more.

The archive work is of particular interest as it will feature, amongst other records and information, the names of every single person who lost their lives in service of RAF Bomber Command (57,861 names), which is no mean feat. It will also focus on RAF experiences, stories and tactics as well as the aftermath and rebuilding of European

and British cities and society. The site will boast what will become the UK's tallest war memorial – a 31m high spire (the same length as a Lancaster Bomber wing) which looks down on Lincoln and across to the Cathedral – as well as two peace gardens amongst other architectural edifices. Find out more at: internationalbcc.co.uk

As the years tick by, we begin to lose our direct connection to the events of the past through those who were there and are still with us now. We are lucky that at our memorials and events, veteran members of the RAF, and the other Armed Forces, can still grace us with their presence and regale us with their stories and experiences.

These monuments and memorials are of paramount importance, as is our support of them, for with no understanding of the past, how can we plot an effective future? It is up to the public to honour the sacrifices of those who came before us and to know our shared histories.

Visiting these monuments and supporting those who maintain and build them is just the first step, it is up to us to carry their stories forward to newer generations so that what we many owe to The Few is not lost to the shadows of history. To find out how you can support the RAF and its memorials, visit: www.rafbf.org

SPECTACULAR AIRSHOWS

The RAF air shows are entertaining for the public and important for publicity and recruitment

Words George Prescott

During the summer in Britain, RAF airshows attract huge crowds, with acrobatic displays and veteran WWII aircraft a speciality. The entry price is not huge, usually between £20-£25, and this often includes all children under 16, as well as a certain amount of free parking. Once in the viewing enclosure, visitors can see acrobatic and flying displays by the RAF display team of the Red Arrows, the Typhoon (Eurofighter) display team, the Battle of Britain Memorial Flight, flying Spitfires, Hurricanes and a Lancaster. Static displays also include aircraft currently in use by the RAF and other airforces as well as the famous types of the Memorial Flight. Not all RAF Air Stations can mount displays but those that do include RAF Cosford (near Wolverhampton), RAF Scampton (near Lincoln) and RAF Fairford, in Gloucestershire, with the Royal International Air Tattoo.

ROYAL INTERNATIONAL AIR TATTOO

Breitling Jet Team at Fairford during the Royal International Air Tattoo on 10 July 2014

The first Air Tattoo was staged at North Weald Airfield in Essex in 1971, becoming the International Air Tattoo in 1976 and the Royal International Air Tattoo in 1996. The Tattoo moved to its present location, RAF Fairford, in 1985 and the event has been staged their ever since, except in 2000 and 2001. The Tattoo is a showcase for the world's military, and has become an important precursor to the Farnborough Airshow which takes place a week after RIAT, on every 'even' year. It allows the military aerospace industry to display its products away from the commercial pressures of the Farnborough show.
DATE OF NEXT SHOW: 13,14,15 July 2018 **LOCATION:** RAF Fairford, Fairford, Gloucestershire, GL7 4EG

The Red Arrows Display Team, flying inverted and with smoke on, while training over RAF Scampton, which is their official base (Cpl Andy Benson/MOD)

RAF COSFORD

Cosford's Airshow is the only RAF event officially supported by the Royal Air Force in Britain and has been held on RAF Cosford's airfield since 1978, regularly attracting crowds of 50,000. Attractions include flying and static displays, fun fair rides, concession stands, food outlets and trade stands. The show also raises money for charity as well as being seen as an important RAF recruitment event. The local train operator sells a combined rail and air show ticket at a discount, allowing users direct access on foot to the airshow.

DATE OF NEXT SHOW: 10 June 2018 **LOCATION:** RAF Cosford, Wolverhampton, WV7 3EX

1. Red Arrow Hawk trainer operating as part of the team's two-man fly-past. This is a dangerous manoeuvre, which has resulted in the deaths of at least two pilots **2.** Typhoon being flown at high speed and showing the heat trail from the exhaust, typical of jet aircraft **3.** A Eurofighter Typhoon, climbing steeply during the Farnborough Air Show in 2010. The engine exhaust is visible on the right

RAF SCAMPTON

The first Scampton Airshow since 1991 took place at Scampton on 9 and 10 September 2017, organised by the Royal Air Force Charitable Trust, which is also responsible for the Royal International Air Tattoo. The show was intended to replace the highly successful event at RAF Waddington, which regularly attracted over 135,000 visitors but had to be cancelled because of health and safety concerns.

However, the new show went ahead and proved a major success, with over 50,000 visitors attending. They were able to see 104 aircraft, including a WWII Avro Anson and a modern Typhoon, as well as wing walking and a mock WWI dogfight. Other attractions included period entertainment and flight simulators. Two Battle of Britain veterans, Terry Clark and Johnny Johnson, also attended the event.

DATE OF NEXT SHOW: Another Airshow is proposed for September 2018

LOCATION: RAF Scampton, Scampton, Lincoln,

COSFORD

RAF MUSEUMS

From wartime aircraft to passenger jets and flying boats, the two museums tell the story of the RAF

Words Duncan Evans

There are two official RAF museums you can go visit, one is at Cosford in Shropshire, the other is in north London at Hendon. This latter museum is still open but is being extensively redeveloped to bring the buildings in line with the modern constructions at Cosford and also IWM Duxford.

The Cosford museum occupies a large site, which is why there's room for large aircraft outside the hangars and display buildings. Before you go anywhere, take a gander at the flying seaboat and the massive Nimrod then head inside for over 70 aircraft

on display. There's the Cold War exhibition which features three nuclear bombers from the V-Force, test flight exhibits, a War in the Air exhibition, then the museums collect of transport and training aircraft in Hangar 1. Other aircraft worth looking out for include the Avro Lincoln – the successor to the Lancaster, the stainless steel Bristol Type 188 experimental jet, the fantastic English Electric Lightning, a Messerchmitt Me 262A and more. For all things RAF though, head for the history gallery.

Over in Hendon there are over 100 aircraft on site and make sure you check

out the new exhibition, First World War in the Air. As part of the rebuild the Battle of Britain and Sunderland halls are closed until Spring, so bear that in mind. Ones that are open include the Milestones of Flight building which shows the early years of flying, the Historic Hangars, which are listed buildings and formed part of the old aerodrome, the Aeronauts interactive centre and the Marine Craft collection.

Both museums are open all year from 10am and entry is free. Go to the **www. rafmuseum.org.uk** website for more details on either.

COSFORD: **1.** On an elevated walkway there are information boards as you head towards the English Electric Lightning **2.** The Avro Lincoln was initially designated as a Lancaster variant before being given its own name **3.** Outside the modern hangars and exhibition spaces is a flying boat and also the giant Nimrod **4.** The Gloster Gladiator Mk.1 single seat fight first flew in 1937 and served until the end of the war
HENDON: 1. Large numbers of fighter planes in a dogfight in the First World War in the Air exhibition **2.** The proposed new hall for the Sunderland flying boat will be ready for the RAF 100th anniversary **3.** This is how the entrance to the London museum will look when it is completed

HENDON

Enjoying this RAF book? You may enjoy *The Armourer*

A monthly magazine featuring:

Discover the people and weapons behind the stories

Guide to prices, rare items, auctions and fairs

Latest militaria news, museums, re-enactments and reports

Call **01778 392489** quote ARM/RAF17

Terms and conditions: Print subscription price of £3.99 applies to UK direct debits only. Subscription price available until 31.12.2018.

TRY IT TODAY!

The Armourer
Incorporating *Classic Arms & Militaria*

SUBSCRIBE FROM JUST £3.99

Also available as a digital magazine – read across all devices. For more information go to

www.pocketmags.com/armourer

Or subscribe online

www.armourer.co.uk

COLLECTING RAF MILITARIA

From uniforms to badges, medals to log books, there are many different items for anyone wanting to build a collection

Words Ed Hallett

Aerial photographs are fascinating, just grab a magnifying glass and see what you can spot

With the RAF reaching its 100th birthday, interest in collecting the most junior service has never been higher. It is easy to see why the RAF is so popular amongst collectors: the service has always been at the cutting edge of technology regardless of the era, the uniforms have always had a sartorial elegance and due to its smaller size it has frequently had a budget to buy the best quality kit for its officers and airmen. Added

to all that is the romance of perhaps being the only armed service where success or failure rides on single combat between two men and their machines, the last vestige of the old days of chivalry. It must be said that some of this mystique is justifiable, and some is the result of good story telling, but the fact remains that the RAF is a popular and rewarding topic for the collector and with 100 years of history there is plenty of material out there to suit all budgets.

In very general terms the older the

artefacts the higher the price they can demand. Pre-World War II items are scarce and can be very expensive, World War II objects are frequently more affordable as so many were produced as part of a global conflict whilst Cold War and modern items are even more affordable. It is also usually the case that the closer the object is to the actual flying of aircraft the more desirable it is, therefore flight gear and uniforms belonging to pilots are far more desirable than those worn by ground crew. Most of

Uniforms

The traditional RAF uniform is made of blue-grey cloth and for the formative years of the RAF was worn for everything from parades to maintaining and flying aircraft. Examples dating from before the 1960s are typically made of barathea for officers and serge for airmen. The uniforms worn during World War II were unique in having a tie for other ranks, making them look far smarter than army battledress and both officers and airmen fastened them with brass buttons with a crown over a soaring albatross motif. These uniforms are easy enough to find, the shirts and ties worn with them are more difficult to track down. Airmen's serge uniforms originally had a white cotton label giving details of manufacturer, date and size; officers purchased their uniforms from a tailor and often these have a label with the name and number of their original owner, making an interesting research project. A serge blue grey battledress known as War Service Dress was also produced for use by aircrew and this is scarcer and hence more collectable than the service dress uniform.

The traditional blue-grey uniforms from the 1960s onwards were reserved for parade duties and were made from a man-made fabric with Staybrite buttons that did not need polishing. These uniforms remain

this comes down to scarcity - there are far fewer pilots than ground crew and the older the object the fewer of them there are in circulation, so the higher the prices.

In addition to this, anything that can be directly attributed to a successful and decorated pilot seems to automatically demand a premium, even more so if he was associated with a famous campaign such as the Battle of Britain. On the other end of the spectrum there remain many RAF artefacts that are considerably cheaper than their army equivalents: blue grey 37 pattern webbing is usually much more affordable than army pattern pieces in comparable conditions. With such a wealth of material available, it is worth looking at a few of the main areas of collecting and offering an overview for those starting a collection. Collectors can find RAF militaria at shows, online auction sites and most militaria dealers. There are a small number of specialist dealers that only sell RAF equipment and these often have a selection of the rarer and more desirable items. The Historic Flying Clothing Company is one of these and many of the photographs in this article are reproduced from their site with their kind permission.

1. Officer's service dress was made of a fine barathea cloth and has remained largely unchanged to the present day **2.** The other airman's service dress was made of blue-grey serge wool with brass buttons and a belt **3.** The officer's peaked cap has remained largely unchanged since the earliest days of the RAF (David Farnsworth, The Historic Flying Clothing Company) **4.** A small emergency first aid kit in a rubberised pouch issued to airmen (David Farnsworth, The Historic Flying Clothing Company)

almost unchanged to the present day and are available very cheaply at surplus prices. The collector should look out for original insignia sewn on them, those with medal ribbons being especially worth paying attention to as any with original gallantry ribbons are very collectable, even if comparatively modern.

More recent conflicts such as those in Afghanistan and Iraq have seen the RAF wear standard army camouflage uniforms; as these have no specific RAF markings on the labels, the collector should look out for unique insignia sewn on the sleeves or above the breast pockets. The RAF tactical recognition flash is a square with thick stripes of dark blue and red separated by a narrow light blue stripe.

Flight equipment

Whilst the blue grey uniforms are very iconic, specialist clothing for aircrew holds a particular interest for many. The line between equipment and uniform can be a little blurred but certainly one of the most desirable pieces of specialist uniform is the Irvin jacket. This was actually half of a two-part set with matching trousers. Both were made of leather with sheepskin lining to combat the cold at altitude. Irvin was just one of several manufacturers of these garments and although forever associated with fighter pilots they were actually used by all aircrews, including bomber and transport crews. These jackets are very popular with collectors and numerous reproductions are around to allow those who want to wear one as a piece of fashion to have an affordable alternative to an original. As such the collector needs to do plenty of research and buy from a reputable dealer to avoid being sold a modern replica.

Of all the items relating to the RAF, flight equipment is perhaps the most collectible of them all. It does not seem to matter if they are World War II, Cold War or modern issue, flight gear holds a special appeal to collectors due to their close association with the actual act of flight. Early flying helmets were copied from contemporary motoring helmets and are made of leather. These became increasingly sophisticated as time went on, with special zippered pockets for headphones, clips for goggles and poppers to attach oxygen masks and microphones to. The different patterns have varying degrees of scarceness, but all are popular to collectors and command good prices.

Post-war these leather helmets tended to be replaced by proper flight helmets, often referred to as bone domes, as the RAF moved into the jet age. Again, as these tend to be named to, and sometimes decorated by, a specific pilot they then become much more collectable.

Other flight gear can include emergency

1. Pith helmets were used by the RAF during the early years of World War II and can be easily recognised by the large flash on the puggarre

equipment such as the iconic Mae West; an emergency lifejacket in case an aeroplane ditches into the sea and the inflatable dinghy used by downed pilots awaiting rescue. Wartime lifejackets tend to be yellow whilst post war examples are orange. Smaller items of emergency kit to look out for include silk escape maps. These are maps of enemy territory printed on silk that allowed them to be folded up in to very small packets and carried in a pocket, the silk avoiding the rustling of a paper map which might give away an escaping airman.

Flight suits are another essential piece of flying kit that although in limited use in the early years of World War II, really became popular towards the end of that conflict and into the post-war period. Early flight suits were little more than overalls, but later designs became ever more sophisticated with heating systems, equipment to combat the effects of g-force and more pockets than the average person would know what to do with. Ironically it is the more modern flight suits that are

2. The most impressive items of RAF head dress are the busbys worn by the RAF Bands. This is an interwar example and is very striking

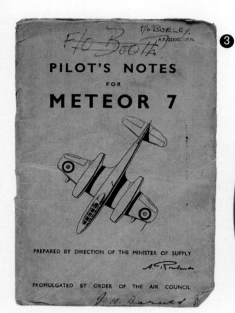

3. Pilot's notes were issued to guide pilots on the idiosyncrasies of a particular type of aircraft (David Farnsworth, The Historic Flying Clothing Company) **4.** Original Operations Room Sector Clocks such as this one are incredibly popular, but cheaper replicas are available (David Farnsworth, The Historic Flying Clothing Company)

actually more interesting, as squadron patches have become commonplace making them more colourful and individualistic than their forbears.

Headgear

RAF officers and other airmen have worn a variety of headwear over the years. Officers have worn a blue grey version of the traditional army officers peaked cap since the founding of the RAF in 1918. Caps dating from World War II are some of the most desirable and have the smaller king's crown badge on the front. Also popular during the war were field service, or side caps. As with their uniforms, officers had high quality privately purchased examples in barathea. By contrast airmen had rougher serge caps, these being still fairly easily found. After the war the standard blue grey beret became the most commonly worn cap, and is still in widespread service today. Early berets can be identified by their larger crowns and the sizing and manufacturer are stamped inside in white ink rather than being a separate label as seen on more recent examples. Both side caps and berets were worn with an RAF cap badge - originally in brass but more recently anodised aluminium Staybrite metal.

Other headgear for the collector to look

for include tropical pith helmets with an RAF flash on the pugaree, slouch hats again with an RAF flash sewn on and specialist parade headgear such as the busby worn by members of the RAF's bands. All of these are rarer and, consequently, more expensive than the peaked and side caps, but offer some welcome variety to a collection.

Station items

The Air Ministry had a habit of marking almost everything it bought for the RAF with a crest and marking and there is a bewildering array of items out there for the collector. Everything from paint brushes to furniture was stamped to show it was owned by the RAF, whilst items such as mess china and cutlery have clear RAF logos on them. I have called these station items because, most commonly, they were seen on RAF bases and fighter stations. Items like an RAF-marked egg cup are a fun and interesting item to have in any collection. They are affordable and perfectly serviceable to use for a boiled egg in the morning. Many of these objects can happily be displayed around the house and enjoyed without upsetting other members of the household. RAF-marked clocks are always popular and many have a subtle RAF badge on the dial face. Larger station sector clocks are

extremely popular and original ones go for very high prices, though more affordable reproductions are available if you cannot justify the prices for an original.

Wooden chairs with large arms can often been seen in period pictures with pilots relaxing in them. Today these chairs make an excellent occasional chair, that actually has some history attached to it, for a study. A number of specialist dealers in RAF militaria have them for sale and this saves the difficulty of searching through thousands of second-hand chairs until you actually find a marked example.

Often with marked station objects the only thing you need to add them to your collection is a keen eye and patience. Look out for anything marked 'AM' with either an ink stamp or punched directly into the wood. Often these items are not recognised as being militaria or RAF objects and can be had for a few pounds; with patience a good collection can be built up.

RAF field gear

The RAF used cotton webbing load-bearing equipment right from its earliest years. In 1925 the RAF purchased a modern and complicated personal load-bearing set known as 1925 pattern webbing that was supplied pre-dyed in blue-grey. This set was unique to the Royal Air Force (and the South African Defence Force in khaki). The early webbing set is highly collectible with the rifle ammunition pouches, especially, being extremely scarce. The pistol set is a little easier to find but still presents a fun challenge to the collector in trying to track down all the components.

By contrast, its replacement was a blue-grey version of the contemporary army 37 pattern set and is very easily available with mint condition components being sold for very reasonable sums. The webbing was used by both airman guarding airfields and by the RAF Regiment who were formed during World War II as the service's ground protection force.

The 37 pattern set was the last set produced exclusively for the RAF and since they were superseded during the Cold War the RAF have used identical equipment to the Army, with only hand written markings giving the collector any indication that it is RAF, rather than army issue, kit. Returning to blue grey 37 pattern webbing; a fun challenge for the collector would be to try and get a set and fill it with the correct, marked RAF items for the period. Kit lists are available, but finding some of the smaller items of personal kit with the correct Air Ministry or RAF markings would be difficult.

Ephemera

This is a catch-all term for paper-based collectibles and for those collecting militaria it can include manuals, photographs, letters, official documents and magazines. This is perhaps one of the most overlooked areas of collecting. The objects are frequently easy on the pocket and are a great starting point for a collection.

The Air Ministry took millions of photographs throughout World War II, both for operational reasons and for use in official news releases. Operational photographs can include aerial photographs taken by aircraft over enemy territory which will often have an ink stamp on the rear, indicating they are official Air Ministry images. Depending on the image itself, the collector can follow in the footsteps of the wartime intelligence services which originally interpreted the photographs. Armed with a magnifying glass it is great fun to try and spot anything of military importance. Publicity photographs share the same Air Ministry rubber stamp on the rear and often have a small typed caption that gives some context and a starting point for further research.

Every aircraft used by the RAF has had a set of pilot's notes issued for it, to help the pilot unused to the aircraft's design, layout and handling. These books are highly collectable and even more modern aircraft

1. The Irvin Flying jacket is a heavyweight sheepskin lined leather jacket that provided much needed warmth to aircrew at high altitudes (David Farnsworth, The Historic Flying Clothing Company) **2.** The Sidcot suit was an electrically heated flying suit for use in the cold upper parts of the atmosphere. (David Farnsworth, The Historic Flying Clothing Company)

ones achieve good prices. The books usually have detailed photographs of the inside of the aircraft and the cockpit.

Collectors should have no difficulty finding items to suit their pocket and tastes and with the internet and specialist traders it has never been easier to find these items. For more detailed looks at RAF items, consider subscribing to specialist collecting magazine, *The Armourer*. Whilst there is a natural interest in the RAF in World War II, there is wealth of interesting history and collectibles spanning the Cold War and the War on Terror which will only go up in price as the years move on and would be ideal for those wishing to use their collection as a future retirement fund.

Browse the galleries of carefully researched and superbly crafted historic air combat scenes at

www.flightartworks.com

Photographic prints from £14.99. Canvas prints from £39
ORDER SECURELY ON PC, TABLET OR SMARTPHONE

1936-40 | BATTLE OF BRITAIN

1941-44 | DAMBUSTERS

WWII FIGHTERS | WWII BOMBERS

1944-45 | JET AGE

Commissions: let me make you a unique full-colour composition of your chosen aviation experience. Editors' and publishers' enquiries welcome.

gary@flightartworks.com 01206 503518 Colchester. Essex. UK

@flightartworks. and read the fascinating stories behind the pictures at www.aerialcombat.co.uk

Midland Air Museum

Coventry Airport
CV3 4FR

Sir Frank Whittle Jet Heritage Centre

Open all year round Hangars

Opening Times:

10am to 5pm

*Tea Room
*Large Exhibition

*Well Stocked Shop
*Conferences

*Sit in Vulcan and Argosy
*Large Free Carpark

www.midlandairmuseum.co.uk
CV3 4FRT
Tel:02476301033

Events
Bank Holiday Monday
Open Cockpits

THE AVIATION EXPERIENCE COMPANY

www.theaviationexperiencecompany.co.uk

Flights – Helicopter, light aircraft and historic aeroplanes including RAF Benevolent Fund Tiger Moth Squadron Training flights with the Tiger Moth Experience

Tours – Specialist VIP tours to aviation locations

Simulators – Fast Jet, 737, 747 and A320

Mobile Sim – Scouts/Guides/Cadets/Schools

Charter flights and much more......

Christmas, birthday, corporate or just because!

Gift certificates available on all experiences

Call us on 0845 456 6515

Email: toni@avex.org.uk

York Military Books

We buy Military, Naval & Aviation books in any quantity from single items to whole collections.

Tel: 01423 360828
Mob: 07717 155619

www.yorkmilitarybooks.co.uk

"A Wonderful Aircraft" tells the story of the DHC Beaver AL Mk1 aircraft's service in various theatres including UK, BAOR, Aden, Malaysia, Kenya, Cyprus and Northern Ireland with the British army between 1960 and 1989.

In A4 paper back of 200 pages including many maps, diagrams and 16 pages of colour and B&W photographs. Only £9 inc. postage (UK only)

Contact: davidkellock@live.co.uk
Or send a cheque to David M Kellock 1 Heswall Avenue, Manchester M20 3ER

WOLVERLEY MILITARIA FAIRS

Wolverley Memorial Hall, Wolverley, nr. Kidderminster, Worcestershire, DY11 5TN
(2 miles north of Kidderminster off the A449)

2018 Dates
7th Jan, 11th Feb, 11th March,
15th Apr, 13th May, 10th June, 2nd Sept,
14th Oct, 4th Nov, 2nd Dec
9am - 1.30pm Admission £1.00

FREE VALUATIONS ON ALL MILITARY ITEMS
WE ALSO BUY
Phone: 07816 853878
Like us on Facebook:
www.facebook.com/wolverleymilitariafair/

Militaria HISTORY

For military history **news**, exclusive **competitions**, magazine **subscriptions**, **special offers** and more!

Sign up for our newsletter today at:

www.armourer.co.uk